The Church College in Today's Culture

by

WALDEMAR O. DOESCHER

AUGSBURG PUBLISHING HOUSE
Minneapolis, Minnesota

THE CHURCH COLLEGE IN TODAY'S CULTURE

Scripture quotations are from the Revised Standard Version of
the Bible, copyright 1946 and 1962 by the Division of Christian
Education of the National Council of Churches.

MANUFACTURED IN THE UNITED STATES OF AMERICA

Preface

Some of the chapters in this volume of studies are new, but most of them are revisions of papers and addresses written for various academic occasions over the past thirty years during which I have been concerned with the problems of the Christian college. Chapter V on "The Place of Natural Science in Christian Higher Education" is a slightly revised reprint of my article by that name published in *Theology Today*. In Chapter I, I have also quoted from my article "Wanted: Firebrands" previously published in *The Lutheran Quarterly*.

I express my appreciation to my friend and colleague, Dr. William L. Young, and my esteemed classmate, Dr. Emil F. Wendt, for thinking these studies good enough to print and for their efforts to secure their publication. I wish also to acknowledge the valuable advice given me by Dr. Wendt and to express my appreciation to my secretary, Mrs. Betty Jackson, and to Miss Meredith I. Sigel for their assistance in typing the manuscript.

W. O. Doescher

Contents

Chapter I

CHRISTIAN EDUCATION
IN A
TECHNOLOGICAL AGE

The Revolutionary Character of Technology

Of the forces that have shaped our contemporary world for a century or more, beyond a doubt the most potent and pervasive has been scientific technology. It has radically transformed our intellectual, personal, and practical existence. It produced the industrial revolution and all its portentous aftermath. In both its theoretical and its practical aspects it has altered our intellectual outlook, our cultural preoccupations, our economic practices and institutions, and even our political policies. It has generated new occupations, new social relationships, and new social customs. By exploiting the irrational weaknesses of human nature, scientific technology has also greatly aggravated the chronic evils of mankind and generated new forms of social pathology peculiar to a technological age. Hence it has posed new and difficult problems for religion and ethics.

7

Although these phenomena have hitherto been most severely felt in the West, the home of science, the current world-wide exportation of Western science and technology presages an equally radical impact on the older Eastern cultures and on the remaining culturally retarded and primitive peoples of the world.

Technology — Asset or Liability

Scientific technology, like other human enterprises, is culturally ambivalent: It has proved to be both a great asset and a great liability. On the one hand, it provides the means to relieve mass poverty, ignorance, and physical misery. It has promoted health, comfort, and release from exhausting toil. On the other hand, by powerfully implementing man's irrational and moral disabilities, his malevolence and sinful passions, scientific technology has intensified the evils that result from man's greed, his lusts, and his pride.

Television, for example, provides a remarkably effective medium of mass communication for the dissemination of useful knowledge, artistic appreciation, and wholesome diversion; but these potential assets are all too frequently nullified by commercial greed and cultural philistinism, which debase the medium by crass commercialism and uninhibited exhibition of crime, violence, and lust. Its corrupt influence is currently reflected in the alarming rise of adolescent crime and immorality.[1]

Likewise, the same science that has brought relief to human suffering and increased human longevity through the advance of medicine, has devised armaments so terrible that their use in modern warfare threatens the annihilation of human civilization.

While scientific technology thus makes the disciplinary and restraining hand of religion and ethics indispensable, it tends, ironically enough, to undermine religious and ethical convictions when they are most needed. Yet the persistent zeal to exploit the prestige of science to the disparagement of religion has merely served to compel man to face up to his real predicament: that *man's supreme and unsolved problem is himself.* Man has become a physical giant while remaining a spiritual pygmy.

The Need of the Hour

Several generations ago, when Matthew Arnold declared that the great desideratum of modern life was "to make reason and the will of God prevail," many thought the remark quaint and somewhat naive. But "to make reason and the will of God pre-

---

[1]cf. "Parents, Children, and Television," Dept. of Research and Survey, National Council of Churches in U.S.A., 1954. See also "Menace of the Movies," by Fred Eastman, *Christian Century*, Jan.-Feb. 1930; the Report by C. C. Morrison in *The Pulpit*, 1953.

vail" was then, and is now, the problem of the hour.
If anything, for us the hour is near, and time is run-
ning out. The "reason" and "the will of God" in
question are not alternatives, but complementaries.
The "reason" meant is simply man's integral cognitive capacity to apprehend the will of God. To use
Prof. Tillich's phrase, it is *"ecstatic,"* not *"technical,"*
reason that is involved. It is the reason that has been
illuminated to spiritual values, and hence is grasped
by, and addresses itself to, the issues of "ultimate concern": those dealing with the meaning, the potential
values, and the destiny of human existence. Thus
science and technology, despite the sceptical snob-
bery of the apostles of "scientism," have suddenly
made God, religion, the church, *the church college,*
relevant to the modern situation.

Certainly, adequate answers to the above issues
are timely and desperately necessary. Now, Christians believe that Christianity's answer to these problems is adequate and final, that its answer is "reasonable," scientifically tenable, and spiritually persuasive. If so, we have a perspective from which to judge
the relevance of Christian higher education to the
perplexities of modern life.

I have said that science and technology have posed
new problems for religion and ethics. What are some
of these? I shall not discuss the grave external effects
of scientific technology, important as they are: the
problems caused by industrialism, labor tensions,
economic conflict, inflation, business depressions,

communism, the cold war. Let me discuss, instead, the inner, more subtle modifications of personality and attitude that characterize the modern inhabitant of technical suburbia.

The Atrophy of God-Consciousness

One consequence of man's immersion in an urban and technological environment is the atrophy of man's mystical sensitivity and, in consequence, the dominance of the illusion of a man-made world.

Modern man lives in a world of human contrivance. He wanders through an "asphalt jungle" amidst canyons of concrete and steel wherein the stars—which hitherto have eloquently declared the glory of God —are blotted out by the glare of electric lights and neon signs. Everywhere he sees human gadgets that attest man's ingenuity, man's power, man's self-sufficiency: phonographs, radios, television receivers, motor cars, diesel trucks, bulldozers, automatic washers, locomotives, jet airplanes, hydroelectric generators. These triumphs of applied science all declare the glory of man.

Living thus in an artificial world, man becomes estranged from nature—where the handiwork of God is more readily discerned. The spectacle of the starry heavens, the majestic mountains, the rolling prairies, the green meadows and cool woodlands, the leaves of autumn, the blossoms of spring, the lonely horizons of the ocean—these aspects of nature have hitherto in all ages inspired the mystic sense of standing in the presence of God.

By comparison, it is psychologically more difficult to feel the presence of God in the clatter and clank of the steel plant, the madhouse of an expressway traffic jam, the roar of the subway train. Everything reminds us of man; little reminds us of God. So God, by a kind of negative habituation, becomes obscured, passes out of man's daily consciousness, and is forgotten and ignored. This decline of the sense of mystic communion with nature and the atrophy of God-consciousness and of religious intuition are related phenomena. Together they reflect themselves in the emotional feebleness and the spiritual shallowness that characterize modern man's esthetic and religious life.

The Outlook for Religion

Now, the question these reflections suggest is this: Are these impediments to vital and whole-souled religion insurmountable? If they are, and if we agree that it is highly improbable that a technological culture can be abandoned, the outlook for religion would be gloomy indeed. Religion would be doomed to die of spiritual asphyxiation. But such a conclusion does not reckon with the fact that religion expresses the deepest needs of human nature. As St. Augustine put it, "Thou hast made us for thyself, O God, and man's heart is restless until it finds its rest in thee." Technology may atrophy, but it cannot extinguish the religious sense.

It is precisely here that Christian culture, for the promotion of which Christian higher education exists, fits into the needs of the hour. What is needed is not only the cultivation of attitudes of prayer, reverence, humility, hope, and adoration; not only the continuous sensitization of conscience that results from habitual contemplation of the beauty of holiness; not only the knowledge and the intellectual skill that can give reasons for the faith that is in us. These aspects of the religious life are indispensable, but they fall short of the needs of technological man because they presuppose precisely what technological man does not generally have: a vivid awareness of the living God. What is needed is nothing short of a spiritual break-through which can revive a vital and passionate God-consciousness in the midst of a mechanistic and technological world. Can man come to feel the presence of God in the steel mill, the hydroelectric generating plant, the diesel locomotive, the transatlantic jet plane? To do so requires attaining—so to speak—a spiritual second wind.

Having interposed the "works of man" between man and God and thus seemingly obscured God from modern vision, we need to discover again with shocked surprise that God refuses to be excluded. "The true Shekinah," said the venerable St. Chrysostom, "is Man." Man, the creator of culture, science, and technology, is impressive. But greater than man,

the creator, is the Creator of man. That God's creature, man, has harnessed the forces and laws of nature to his purpose is indeed impressive. But more
impressive is the sublime Power by whose word the
heavens were made, the earth and the laws and
forces thereof. Else man would have nothing to bend
to his purpose. So God is there all the while—creatively present in the man who creates, in the creative
capacities man possesses, in the laws and forces of
nature that he exploits. Carlyle prophesied truly
when he said, "A splendor of God, in one form or
other, will have to unfold itself from the heart of
these our Industrial Ages too: or they will never get
themselves organized; but continue chaotic, dis-
tressed, distracted evermore, and have to perish in
frantic suicidal dissolution."[2]

I take this to be one of the important services that
Christian culture as fostered in Christian colleges
must render to our generation; namely, to nurture a
new charismatic community of the redeemed within
our society which is aware of the "splendor of God"
amidst an industrial and technological environment,
and which can communicate that vision to others.

The Existential Boundaries of Life

Another effect of the technological age is its tendency to induce evasion of the existential boundaries
of human existence. The philosophical attitude called

---

[2]*Past and Present,* Book IV, Ch. 1.

"existentialism" disparages an abstract intellectualism. For existentialism, thought is a factor in the dynamics of existence in which we are inextricably involved, and which imposes on us the necessity of continuous, fateful decisions, through which existence itself and, with it, our personal destinies are shaped and determined. Yet this call to a life of free and responsible decision must not induce man to evade the realities of finite human existence. Only that kind of life is genuine and authentic which knows and accepts these stark boundaries of our finitude.

Existentialists endeavor to be radically honest in reporting the facts of life. They refuse both to denigrate human nature and to apotheosize it. However, in discharging this task of reporting the existential facts of life with ruthless honesty, the existentialists call our attention to disabilities and evils much more profound and more serious than those ordinary "ills that flesh is heir to," which concern the social reformer. In comparison with the so-called existential determinants of life, the evils of poverty, unemployment, ill health, crime, vice, even political injustice are transient and tolerable. These resolution and courage can mitigate. The existentialists are concerned rather with that invincible malaise that is rooted in our very finitude and our perversity. These facts define the ultimate limits of human existence. We must live with them; we cannot change them or evade them. Jaspers calls them "the boundary situations" of human existence.

The first of these "boundary situations" is *finitude* itself. I never find within myself the grounds of my own existence. I am radically dependent on a transcendent power that confers existence upon me. Nothing necessitates or requires my existence. There is therefore no cogent reason why I now exist or should continue to exist. Not only is my existence absolutely dependent on a transcendent source, but it is at the same time radically contingent, frail, and precarious. I continue to exist at the suffrance of this power, which remains inscrutable and unpredictable. Therefore, I am not my own, I am not self-sufficient, *I am in no sense master of my fate*. The conditions of my existence are not in my control. I might seek to defy, but I cannot evade, this radical finitude, creatureliness, and dependence under which I must live. I live on a thin crust that covers an abyss of nothingness which at any moment may collapse and threaten me with total annihilation. This consciousness of one's feeble hold on existence and the prospect of imminent dissolution can never be wholly evaded. It is present as an undertone of grim *anxiety* beneath the normal and more superficial concerns of human existence.

Another one of Jaspers' "boundary situations" is luck or *happenstance*. It is our luck (good or ill) to have been "thrown" into our time, place, or circumstance. Heidegger calls this "Geworfenheit." Moreover, life moves cautiously between innumerable unknown and unpredictable hazards. The chances of good or ill fortune constantly upset our rational prudence, our planning, our control of life's issues. Much of this appears to us as arbitrary and meaningless, productive of astonishing coincidence, paradox, absurdity, grotesque irony. We live in *dread* of such unpredictable hazards. "Insurance," or other such secular palliatives, may try to soften the impact, but they cannot prevent their occurrence.

A third "boundary situation" is *suffering*. To be human, existentialists warn us, is to suffer. It is an inescapable ingredient of life. Much of it is due to man's own inhumanity to man, but much of it is natural, a built-in feature of terrestrial life. There is both physical and mental suffering. Only the latter is peculiar to human existence and is possible because of the personalistic structure of human nature. Both the spectacle and the experience of suffering produce fear and recoil. No one can escape. It is a cross that must be borne as the price of being human. It is only a question whether we can bear it willingly and courageously, or reluctantly and rebelliously.

Another "boundary situation" is *frustration*. By this existentialists do not mean only the normal instances where insurmountable obstacles defeat our purposes. They mean the more radical defeats which result from *man's self-transcending aspirations*. This, too, is peculiar to human existence. We find in ourselves capacities that demand fulfillment and perfection. We know, but we never know enough; we aspire, but our reach always exceeds our grasp; we plan the perfect work, but there is always a flaw; we love, but never with utter self-abandon and perfect fidelity, we have high hopes, but they are bound to be shattered; we need time, but there is never time enough. Thus, paradoxically, we find ourselves endowed with ideal aspirations incommensurate with the structure of reality. So we come to the end of life with unfulfilled hopes, with unfinished tasks, with wasted opportunities, with frustrated yearnings for a perfection which we feel our nature demands but which the brutal facts deny. Thus is life shadowed by an inescapable sense of frustration and doom.

Jaspers' fifth "boundary situation" is *guilt*. It is important to note that both religious existentialists like Kierkegaard, Buber, Jaspers, and Marcel and atheistical existentialists like Sartre and Heidegger agree that an ineradicable feeling of guilt belongs to the phenomenological description of human existence. In both groups guilt results from consciousness of our moral infidelity, our betrayal of ultimate reality. In Sartre, however, this can mean only a violation of the fiat of my own will whereby I myself must confer dignity and authenticity upon my life. Now, guilt is essentially shame and loss of self-respect. Christians marvel that God should condescend to love "such a worm as I," and conventional men of the world have only amused contempt for such attitudes of self-abasement. Nothing, in their opinion, calls for such a confession of shame and guilt. But what is so much of our present *outré* literature, with its cynical human self-disparagement and its nauseating exhibition of human depravity, but just such a confession of guilt, modern style? In Buber and Jaspers, such guilt is founded on consciousness of disloyalty to God, from whom I draw my existence and whose will is the objective standard and foundation of all good. In acknowledging as an inescapable fact man's propensity to evil and the universality of the sense of guilt and moral unworthiness, the existentialists have rediscovered so-called "original sin" and have, with unexpected sophistication, returned to the moral realism of the Bible.

The final "boundary situation" is *death*. This goes beyond the anxiety attached to the uncertain hazards of our existence; it is born of the knowledge that death is inevitable and imminent and that *per se* it threatens the total extinction of personality. It is difficult for us to take death with existential seriousness. "All men are mortal" is general, abstract, remote. It is the major premise of a classical syllogism that hardly disturbs our peace of mind. If one were to say to us, "Tomorrow morning at 4 A.M. you die," it would give us an existential jolt. In real life such a statement in the second person would incite terror. Death is the ultimate terror, not merely because it destroys values but because it destroys the being for which values exist. Good is not good unless it is "good for something" and, above all, good for somebody. Death, if it is the last word, announces the

bankruptcy of a rational universe. Man is the only
being on earth who knows that he must die.

The prospect of such *total* devaluation, of the re-
duction of what has the highest worth to worthless
nothingness, is the most absurd of life's paradoxes
from which man recoils with feelings of desolation
and despair. Existentialists reject the purely naturalistic view of death as the mere cessation of physiological functioning, on the basis of which we are
bidden to die good-humoredly as one "who wraps
the draperies of his couch about him and lies down
to pleasant dreams." Animals can die naturally, but
this is impossible for man. Deep down man is convinced that, for a person, death is "unnatural." It is
"the final enemy." The naturalistic view callously
ignores the radical character of this showdown conflict between being and nothingness, between meaning and meaninglessness, between personal value and
impersonal worthlessness. Hence our life is haunted
by the ominous shadow of death and the secret
terror and *despair* which this shadow evokes. Existentialists insist that only that life is honest and "authentic" which has fully confronted these ultimate
and inexorable determinants of human existence.

Now, by comparison life in Suburbia ignores these
stark realities behind a facade of pleasant illusions
and studied evasions. It evades the accusations of
guilt and the acceptance of moral responsibility by
a shallow and trivial view of the moral life. Knowing
nothing of the shattering demands of radical justice,

radical love, and radical courage, it boasts of its feeble virtues, ignores its own hypocrisies, and lapses into easy self-complacency and self-righteousness. It studiously shuns inconvenience and avoids conflict. It is embarrassed by the obscene improprieties of nature.

Old age, for example, which is man's ripening for the grave, is desperately banished behind the masquerade of perpetual youth. It is zealously disguised by liberal applications of cosmetics, wave sets, and bridgework. The tragic solemnity of the life-cycle is but feebly felt. The melancholy mystery and pain of birth are hidden behind the obstetrical facade of the delivery room, from which fathers are strictly excluded. The tragedy of dying and the stark ministration that once required men to contemplate the hideousness of human dissolution are now consigned to the secret chambers of the professional mortician. Man cannot bring himself to look on the ultimate facts of life with unaverted gaze.

The surface of life is choked with a multitude of mediocre concerns. With Mr. Prufrock one ponders earth-shaking issues: "Shall I part my hair behind? Do I dare eat a peach?" Suburbia's wisdom is expressed in its classic maxims: "Don't stick your neck out," "Play it safe," "Keep your shirt on," "So what!" These tepid emotions know neither the desolation of grief nor the exaltation of heroism. Having no capacity to contemplate grandeur, feeling only fitfully

the "tragic sense of life," the dwellers of Suburbia
remain self-confident, unafraid, amiably self-indul-
gent.

> *And the wind shall say: Here were decent*
> > *Godless people:*
> *Their only monument the asphalt road*
> *And a thousand lost golfballs.*[3]

On the problem of how one deals practically with
the above-mentioned "boundary situations," the answer of religious existentialists must obviously be
very different from that of the atheistic existentialists.
The former would say that what is impossible for
man is possible for God. God alone can close the gap
between human aspirations and human impotence,
he alone can deal with the problem of guilt, he alone
can rescue man from the terror of death. Sartre and
Heidegger deny that such divine resource is available. They can, of course, by a fiat of good will as-
suage their self-respect and support humanitarian
causes. They can and do oppose the "abolition of
man."[4] When faced with the existential ultimates—
while acknowledging that they are *not* ultimate mas-
ters of their fate—they still claim that their head is
bloody but unbowed, and shake their fists at the
universe. Thus, by personal decree, they claim to
inject some measure of good into a worthless world,
and then pass into nothingness with dignity and
heroic resignation. But to shake one's fist at the

---

[3]From "Choruses from the Rock," by J. S. Elliot, *Complete
Poems and Plays,* Harcourt Brace & Co., New York; 1952.
[4]cf. C. S. Lewis, *The Abolition of Man,* Macmillan, New York;
1947.

materialistic world-machine is as absurd as shaking one's fist at a cigar-store Indian.

Honesty requires that men face and accept the existential realities of human life and not seek to evade or forget them. But to accept these "boundary situations" on the assumption of atheistic belief is to dissolve at once their existential character. My duty to be honest in a universe absolutely indifferent to honesty becomes meaningless. I cannot take such a duty with existential seriousness. To impose it upon myself, as Sartre suggests, does not attest an essential nobleness in me, since such values are basically unreal in an unconscious and indifferent universe. Such a gesture appears more like an egotistical whim that ignores rather than respects reality. The only true solution to the existential paradoxes is given by Christian faith, which presents an existential solution for man's existential predicament. God *acts* to redeem man. He does not reveal a new gnosis. In this act God invites men to join a creative crusade, to enlist in an adventurous treasure-hunt, not merely to read a description or a prospectus. And men must respond by personal commitment, not by mere assent to dogma. To nurture a community wherein men can be inspired to make such a commitment is the function both of the church and the church college. They have here a common task, namely, *to make Christian living socially pervasive and effective in all avenues of life.* And this they can do more successfully as partners than as independent institutions.

Chapter II

CHRIST AND CULTURE:
FRIENDS OR ENEMIES

I have suggested that it is the duty of the church to foster higher education in order to make Christian living socially pervasive and effective amidst the unprecedented conditions and special difficulties of a technological age.

This view has not gone unchallenged. The title of this chapter is, in part, borrowed from a recent book of H. Richard Niebuhr's, *Christ and Culture*. The juxtaposition of the terms suggests the problem of their proper relationship. Are they friends or enemies? Behind this question there lurks the lingering doubt whether the church is, after all, a proper proponent of culture, civilization, and general enlightenment. Is there not a danger that the church, in thus actively promoting a rich and congenial earthly existence, will be diverted from her great commission of calling men to repentance and faith through the Gospel? Will the concern for the blessings of our earthly vocation dim the vision of our heavenly destiny? Will time crowd out eternity? Will Christianity degenerate into urbane worldliness and the Gospel of a transcendent redemption be reduced to a pseudo-gospel of immanent human perfectibility?

The View That Christ Opposes Culture

These questions, I believe, are largely a consequence of a mistaken dichotomy between the natural and the supernatural, between the secular and the sacred—a dichotomy that dominated the medieval outlook in the so-called "medieval synthesis" but whose effects lingered on in certain forms of Protestantism. The highest ideal of the medieval synthesis was monasticism, the organization of other-worldly asceticism. In this view Christ opposes culture and must destroy it. Culture—by which we mean the material, ethical, esthetic, and intellectual activities of historic civilizations—is "of this world," tainted with sin, under divine wrath, wholly incompatible with Christ's kingdom, which is "not of this world." Hence, the true Christian who has the courage to follow the highest way of heroic renunciations denies the world, home, wife, children, economic, political, and civic pursuits, and retreats to the solitude of a monastic cell, or the exclusiveness of the conventicle—to await, through prayer and meditation, his translation into the world to come.

This solution was rejected by Luther and the Reformers as incompatible with the biblical understanding of life. It dismisses history and man's historic vocation—not indeed as illusion in the manner of Hinduism or Neo-Platonism—but as a theater of creaturely activity condemned and abandoned by God. Historical existence is not even the raw material of a kingdom of God—it has become the kingdom of the devil.

Such a view seriously impairs any proper view of God's sovereign rule over his creation. That the very principle of historic existence must be repudiated cannot be consonant with belief in God as Creator and Lord of history. This would nullify God's purpose in creating man, subjecting him to the time order, placing him on earth equipped with creative capacities that are the image of his Maker, and commanding him to labor and to have dominion over the earth.

The ascetic view clearly contravenes, also, the radical implications of the incarnation for the understanding of history. God's redemptive purpose works *through* and *in* history and in no other way. It does not seek to short-circuit the historic process—for all its finitude, its frustrations, and its sinful taint which calls down upon it the wrathful judgment of God. The Word became flesh, with all its weakness and frailty, subject to the relativities of time, place, and local custom; subject too, to the vindictive malevolence and destructiveness of human sin. Thus Christ humbled himself—to meet the problem of evil, not by transcending history, but by means of the forces and resources that genuinely move history. Thus the incarnation is our supreme warrant for taking history and historic vocation seriously.

Moreover, there is implied in the doctrine of man as God's creature a doctrine of stewardship of talents. Jesus said, "Unto whomsoever much is given, much is required," and I take this to be a universal truth. It defines for each the seriousness of life and of one's calling. Socially it imposes on nations, and upon social institutions generally, the fulfillment of some valid historic mission. Failure to apply all one's talents creatively to the opportunities afforded by one's time and place is a sinful neglect of the good gifts of God. Not in vain—nor certainly as a sinful delusion and a snare—has the Lord endowed man with reason, intelligence, esthetic feeling, imagination, moral conscience. These define capacities whose creative manifestations must generate the great categories of culture—science, learning, art, law, and morality. In these things everything is exhibited that is distinctively human, everything that lifts man above the level of the beast. To set a genuine value upon these human activities, when man is thus most himself, most human, is the substance of true humanism.

Christ and Culture As Compatible

Ideally, there is no tension between Christ and culture. Yet the very title of Niebuhr's book, *Christ and Culture*, suggests such an antithesis. Now, I admit that there is a tension; a tension, too, as Luther saw, which can never be completely resolved but only mitigated in this earthly life. But it is a tension between Christ and sin, between God and creaturely egocentrism, not a tension between Christ and any valid culture—for Christ does not oppose truth, nor beauty, nor moral authority.

This tension is a consequence of man's sinful self-preoccupation. He labors for the glory of man, generic or specific, not for the glory of God. Thus man's culture is often corrupt, a monument to human pride and selfishness. Its knowledge and its techniques are exploited by the lust for power, glory, wealth, and pleasure. But the true cure for this cultural pathology is not renunciation of the world and culture, not its relegation to the kingdom of the devil. The true cure, it seems to me, is a bold move to claim *all* for the glory of God and his Christ. Christians must labor to produce a Christian culture even though doomed forever to fall short of this ideal. Here "not failure but low aim is crime."

Christ, then, is no enemy of true culture. We could certainly say that historic precedent favors this view. For 2,000 years the church has been a patron of culture. It has inspired free government, humane institutions, education and enlightenment, moral and social idealism, great poetry, painting, architecture, music, philosophy, and theology. A vital Christian church has always been a culturally creative church. Conversely, a church that refuses to appropriate the whole of life for Christ, that disparages intelligence, trifles with truth, and lacks passion for beauty and justice—that church is moribund and in the death-throes of ecclesiastical provincialism. Certainly the church of the Reformation, which, we like to boast, was "born in a university" has a special obligation to cherish and hand down her great cultural tradition.

There are, however, better reasons than loyalty to historic tradition why the church must be a patron of liberal culture. I hold that *this is really a religious duty and a necessary form of Christian piety.* Nothing short of this is involved in the exhortation: "You, therefore, must be perfect, as your heavenly Father is perfect," and in the parable of the talents. These show us that the ideal of human perfection, the aspiration to realize man's highest capacities, is an *obligation involved in the stewardship of life and of human talents.*

It is contemptuous of God to devaluate human nature, carelessly to waste and neglect its immense possibilities for truth, beauty, and goodness, or the manifold opportunities and duties of our earthly existence. He who would revere in every man, including himself, the image of his Maker, would certainly be bound to make that image as explicit as possible by eliminating from it the defects of ignorance, capriciousness, callousness, and irreverence. This is precisely what a liberal and Christian culture attempts to do as a duty toward God.

The same conclusion follows when the Christian

considers his duty toward man and society. Never
before have we been compelled so clearly to realize
the world's need of spiritual convictions and devotion to the higher values and purposes of life. Unless
we succeed in inciting a degree of good will that is
commensurate with man's present technical mastery
of material nature, human civilization will presently
be reduced to shambles.

To prevent this the church college must contribute
its effort to provide our world with a new leadership,
with men of steadier purpose, deeper insight, and
more profound human sympathy. The church has
long recognized the obligation to promote good cit-
izenship. But in our day, in a democratic society,
this means the duty to provide the proper type of
education, an education that will foster mature personality, high ideals, and a true sense of values.

The Christian college, dedicated to fostering liberal culture, far from being an expensive luxury, is
thus seen to be a vital and indispensable confession
of the church's faith. It is a necessary expression of
Christian love: love to God and love to our fellow
man.

The Idea of Christian Culture

Obviously this claim implies that the culture we
have in mind is *Christian* culture. I should like to
insist that there *is* such a thing, and that its promotion is a Christian obligation.

Christian culture would differ from our contemporary culture, which is the heir of the Renaissance, not in its subject matter and its fields of creative activity, but in its presuppositions and motivations. Christian culture repudiates the secular and man-centered point of view, the glorification of the creature, that the Renaissance instigated. Instead, it would restore a theocentric approach to life. Cultural activity would then be carried on for the glory of God, not for the vanity of man.

This shift to a theocentric attitude would not exclude a thoroughgoing, though Christian, humanism, nor dry up the wellsprings of inspiration, as some have feared. For such a theocentric, or theonomous, culture would not again—since the Reformation—return to the condition of ecclesiastical regimentation. It was the revolt against a repressive church regime, which was unable, so to speak, to domesticate the humanistic movement, that resulted in the excesses of the Renaissance and instigated the secularism and anticlericalism of the Enlightenment which we have largely inherited. The only antidote to these tendencies is for the evangelical churches boldly to promote a theocentric culture. Such a culture can readily and consistently espouse natural science, literature, art, music, and politics, for Christianity believes that nature and man, having been created by God, are worthy of reverence in all their aspects and manifestations.

Almost a century ago a great Christian scholar and

gentleman—John Henry Newman—set down his conception of a university. What I have tried to say about the church college as a cultural community may fittingly be concluded by some words of that eloquent Oxonian:

> *A University is a place of concourse whither students come from every quarter for every kind of knowledge. You cannot have the best of every kind everywhere; you must go to some great emporium for it. . . . In the nature of things, greatness and unity go together; excellence implies a center. And such is a University. It is a place to which a thousand schools make contributions; in which the intellect may safely range and speculate, sure to find its equal in some antagonist activity, and its judge in the tribunal of truth. It is a place where inquiry is pushed forward, and discoveries verified and perfected, and rashness rendered innocuous, and error exposed, by the collision of mind with mind, and knowledge with knowledge. It is the place where the professor becomes eloquent, and is a missionary and a preacher, displaying his science in its most complete and most winning form, pouring it forth with the zeal of enthusiasm, and lighting up his own love of it in the breasts of his hearers. . . . It is a place which wins the admiration of the young by its celebrity, kindles the affections of the middleaged by its beauty, and rivets the fidelity of the old by its associations. It is a seat of wisdom, a light of the world, a minister of the faith, an Alma Mater of the rising generation.[1]*

It would seem incredible indeed if the Christian faith could not adopt as its own so noble a vision!

---

[1]"Rise and Progress of Universities," J. H. Newman in *Selections from the Prose Writings*, ed., L. E. Gates, Holt, New York; 1895.

Chapter III

THE VALUE OF THE CHRISTIAN COLLEGE

We have suggested that Christian culture is more necessary than ever and that its chief patron is the Christian college. But we cannot defend the Christian college in the abstract, since there are such wide differences in particular colleges. The only kind of Christian college worth defending is one that is properly equipped to carry out its educational ideal in practice. Such a college must have adequate material equipment in the form of buildings, laboratories, and libraries; it must have a competent and scholarly faculty; it must be administered by men and women of real spiritual life and conviction. When the college falls below these minimum standards it is hardly worth the trouble, in my opinion, to keep it alive. Our standardizing agencies, such as the North Central Association, are perfectly justified in saying: Either become intellectually respectable or get out of business. Otherwise the whole business of denominational education will fall into disrepute among intelligent people.

Denominational Education

Now, it is this phrase, "denominational education," that deserves a moment's reflection. There are social philosophers, like Mr. Bertrand Russell, who do not hesitate to say that such a phrase is a contradiction in terms, and in this he is espousing a view that is widely popular at the present time. "This immersing the defenseless younger generation in the atmosphere of faiths, religious and political," it is charged, "makes them *partisans* rather than unprejudiced truth seekers." Is it right to impose beliefs upon uncritical and immature minds? Is it not better to encourage minds to come to their own conclusions, by the impartial presentation of all points of view? These are the questions that are asked. And since the denominational college is committed to a single point of view to the exclusion of all others, does it not by imposing its beliefs upon young minds make them little more than echoes of its institutional life, incapable of appreciating any truth outside of their own denominational boundaries? These, we must admit, are weighty questions that need to be faced squarely.

Let me say at once that there is considerable exaggeration in the way the question is thus usually put. No denominational college with an intelligent faculty fosters its point of view by mental coercion and dogmatizing, mechanically stuffing the heads of its hapless students with stereotyped formulas. Such methods of teaching doubtless exist, but let me say here from considerable experience that they are by no means confined to the denominational college. No, the denominational colleges, too, *make the appeal to intelligence and reason and moral insight even in matters of faith.* They, too, practice objective exposition and utilize rational persuasion rather than propaganda appeal.

In the second place, the criticism exaggerates the degree of divergence in point of view between the denominational college and a non-denominational or state institution. It is nonsense to contend that the distinctive point of view to which a Christian college is committed alters any facts over the whole wide field of knowledge. Nine-tenths of the facts of knowledge belong to the educational *adiaphora*, if I may borrow a term from theology, i.e. to things whose relationship to intelligent faith is neutral or noncrucial. That remaining one-tenth, to be sure, is crucial: It involves nothing less than a complete philosophy of life which implicates and commits the whole personality. While, therefore, it is eminently true that the dogmas of religious faith constitute the basis of the distinctive point of view of the church college and its faculty, and as such determine the ends and methods of educational policy, it is also true that as

mere items in the facts of instruction they are in the
minority and not in the majority, since no church
college teaches the tenets of a particular religion and
nothing else. Factually there is no more theistic
chemistry than there is atheistic chemistry. There is
only chemistry. Christian faith will indeed reflect
itself in the attitude of the professor and in his general presuppositions, but it changes no facts.

Thirdly, let us note that the commitment of the
Christian college to a special point of view is not at
all a radical or subversive principle but merely the
extension of a principle that lies at the basis of all
education whatsoever: that there is a system of objective truth which needs to be communicated to
young minds if they are to live the best possible life.
It is unfortunately true, of course, that some truths
that we accept as indisputable and vital are denied
to be such by others. But that does not alter the
principle that once you have accepted a fact as true
objectively and absolutely, you are bound to be a
protagonist for that truth until it prevails. Not, be it
noted again, prevails irrationally and mechanically, but rationally; the *grounds of which may be eluci-
dated and shown sufficient to convince a reasonable
mind.*

There is much loose talk nowadays about the virtue
of holding all possible points of view. No self-respec-
ting intellect entertains all possible points of view
about everything: Such a consummation of liberal-
ism is possible only for maniacs and imbeciles. One

cannot be "broadminded" about the binomial theorem. There would seem to be two types of facts about which we entertain different points of view: values or personal tastes, and speculations or hypotheses. Disputes about personal tastes, as for example whether roses are more beautiful than violets, are notoriously inconclusive, and we usually decide the matter with a proverb: *De gustibus non disputandum est*—there is no use arguing about tastes.

Speculations and hypotheses, on the other hand, imply a state of intellectual suspended animation. The evidence is inconclusive. We cannot decide, we have no convictions, hence we can equally entertain various points of view. But now take such items as are universally accepted as objectively valid. We never think of teaching other points of view on such matters as that 2x2 equals 4, that Napoleon fought the Battle of Waterloo, that Columbus discovered America, that fire burns. To be sure, even in teaching such facts we never hand them down as sheer brute dogmas, but we appeal to insight and understanding. But, once more, so does the man who teaches what he takes to be a religious fact. Like all good teachers, he presents his case, not by ignoring opposing points of view, but by proving them defective compared with his own. The demand that a teacher should not be a propagandist is at bottom a demand that he have no convictions—and this I do not hesitate to call pedagogical nonsense.

The Justification of the Denominational College

The justification of the denominational college, therefore, resolves itself to this: It takes the fact of God and his redemptive action in history so seriously that it is willing *to assume the responsibility of treating it as an objective fact* that can be commended to the young mind before that mind is able to evaluate it critically.

Let us never suppose that educators can escape this responsibility. It is a superficial notion that young minds are able to weigh critically the merits of different points of view, before they are equipped with a certain body of facts, experiences of life, and critical standards of judgment. Where this theory is held, the results are usually mere superficial cleverness and intellectual befuddlement. Let me quote some wise and weighty remarks on this subject by a profound American thinker, Professor Hocking, of Harvard:

> *Children have rights which education is bound to respect. The first of these rights is not that they may be left free to choose their way of life, i.e. to make bricks without either straw or clay. Their first right is that they be offered something positive, the best the group has so far found. Against errors and interested propaganda the growing will has natural protection: it has no protection against starvation, nor against the substitution of inferior food for good food. No social authority can make pain appear pleasure. No social authority can make a stimulus of something that has no value. But it is quite*

possible, through crowding out the better by the worse, to produce a generation which thinks push-pin as good as poetry, prefers bridge to sunsets, or worships the golden calf.[1]

There is, then, an unavoidable exercise of authority in all education, whether we like it or not, an authority which is always coextensive with the range of our most intense convictions. So certain are we of the truth of certain matters that we assume the responsibility of concentrating those truths upon the growing mind with all our powers of persuasion, never doubting that subsequent experience will prove our conviction well founded, or our alleged truth tenable. As long, therefore, as Christians have their distinctive convictions, so long must we acknowledge their right to maintain schools to propagate the truths of which they are convinced.

"No very startling conclusion!" I hear many of you say. Why all this hemming and hawing about the barest of unprofitable negations when we are on fire with the zeal of the Lord? In the midst of this call to heroic service for Christ and his kingdom, why stop to make feeble apologies for our very existence? Alas, that it should be necessary! But I should not have detained you with even feeble apologies if I had not thought it necessary today, not merely to expound the value of the Christian college but to justify its right to exist as a separate institution.

---

[1]*Human Nature and Its Remaking*, W. E. Hocking, Yale University Press, 1918, p. 234.

The Church at the Crossroads

The church of Jesus Christ stands today at one of the most critical junctures of her history. Her creed has for centuries supplied the philosophical orientation of Western culture. Today an expansive and aggressive Communism, espousing the Marxian gospel of dialectical materialism, is boldly throwing down the gauntlet to any and all theistic worldviews. Moreover, within the bounds of nominal Christendom we are witnessing the blatant revival of a new paganism which seeks to reduce Christianity, as did the paganism of imperial Rome, to the status of a *religio licita:* tolerated either as an intriguing esthetic legend among the sophisticated, or as an atavistic superstition among the naive. The hallmark of the new paganism is its secularism, its this-worldliness, its attempt to found upon a bare physical nature and a bare human nature, divorced from God, an adequate conception of Ultimate Reality, and of the meaning and destiny of human life. It is, therefore, predominantly naturalistic and humanistic in temper and is radically opposed to what it calls "supernaturalism" in all its forms. Where this naturalism is not frankly materialistic, as in the case of Mr. Bertrand Russell, it takes the form of a vague pantheistic mysticism, which—if it speaks of "God" at all—conceives him as little more than an impersonal principle-of-order in nature. Either, then, naturalism believes in the supremacy of a "matter" that hands this universe

over to "the trampling march of unconscious power," from whose inexorable tyranny humanity has no
escape; or else, conceding feebly that "God" (after a
fashion) exists, it so identifies him with the visible
universe as to imply, on our part, no responsibility
or commitment whatsoever to a higher Being. Such
a view is doubtless superficially flattering to human
pride and sedative to guilt-plagued consciences. Its
attitude is well expressed in that impertinent parody
of Swinburne's:

"Glory to man in the highest! For man is the master
of things!"

More frequently, however, modern paganism takes
the materialistic alternative which leads man into
the dark morass of pessimism and disillusionment.
Permit me to quote to you a famous utterance of this
sort from a brilliant modern writer, Sir Bertrand
Russell:

> *Purposeless and void of meaning is the world which
> science reveals to our belief. That man is the product of
> causes that had no prevision of the end they were
> achieving, that his origin, his growth, his hopes and
> fears, his loves and beliefs, are but the outcome of
> accidental collocations and atoms; that no fire, no hero-
> ism, no intensity of thought or feeling can preserve an
> individual life beyond the grave, that all the labors of
> the ages, all the devotion, all the inspiration, all the
> noonday brightness of human genius are destined to
> extinction in the vast death of the solar system, and
> that the whole temple of man's achievements must in-
> evitably be buried beneath the debris of universe in
> ruins—all these things, if not quite beyond dispute, are*

yet so nearly certain that no philosophy that rejects them can hope to stand.

For Man, condemned today to lose his dearest, tomorrow himself to pass through the gate of darkness, it remains only to cherish ere yet the day falls, the lofty thoughts that ennoble his little day; and—proudly defiant of the irresistible forces that tolerate for a moment his knowledge of his condemnation, to sustain alone, a weary but unyielding Atlas, the world that his own ideals have fashioned despite the trampling march of unconscious power.[2]

There we have the classic expression of that pathetic and unrelieved gloom that attends materialism's answer to the question of human life and destiny. That such is the ultimate outcome of naturalistic thought is most ably expounded and documented by an eminent social critic, Mr. Joseph Wood Krutch, whose incisive book, *The Modern Temper,* I heartily commend to the reader who cares to pursue this question further.

Christian Ethics Under Attack

Today such corrosive doubts and scepticisms are no longer limited to the doctrinal and intellectual aspects of Christianity, such as the existence of God, the reality of revelation, the destiny of man. Contemporary scepticism, which pervades much of modern ethical philosophy, is now being directed as well against the fundamental principles of Christian morality. Hitherto it was assumed that, whatever else about Christianity was dubious, at least the ethics of

---

[2]"A Free Man's Worship" in *Mysticism and Logic,* by Bertrand Russell, Longmans, New York; 1923; pp. 46-57.

Jesus was beyond serious criticism. Our most distinguished sophist of a generation ago, Mr. H. L. Mencken, was an avowed Nietzschean in morals. He once
wrote a cynical attack on Jesus' teaching on sex morality, on which subject he considered Mr. Freud a
more "scientific" authority. Now, Mr. Mencken, keen
as was his intellect in many ways, was unfortunately
distinguished for his distorted conception of what
Christianity really means from a mature level of
thought. Nevertheless, his sustained attitude of cyni-
cism and satire had the intelligentsia of the day by
the ears. Today, a generation later, the researches of
Prof. Kinsey into the question of prevailing moral
customs has startlingly revealed how far the decay
of Christian morals has gone.

This secular paganism, of which the men to whom
I have alluded are typical, is today quite prevalent
in the colleges and universities of America. To be
sure, religion in many circles is still respected, God
is invoked, and Jesus is admired. Too often, however,
this fashionable religiosity is feeble, tentative, and
without practical personal consequences. The God
who is often invoked in speculative religion as the
conservator of values never descends from his heaven
of metaphysical abstraction. One is reminded of the
Universalist preacher who began his prayer with
the invocation, "To Whom It May Concern!" There
is genuine alarm when one proposes that the authentic voice and word of God has really appeared on
the plane of history and that God has addressed him-

self to the will and intelligence of man. Personally,
I have come to the conclusion that all such notions as
these are polite but veiled forms of atheism, real and
chronic inability to believe in God. While, doubtless,
in many cases such scepticism is due to honest doubt,
much of it, on the other hand, must be interpreted as
a dogmatic obsession that reflects a subconscious
misotheistic complex.

The Sacramental View of Life

In the midst of all this religious anarchy, the Christian college, even with its shortcomings and occasional obscurantism, is an effective exponent of what has been called "the sacramental view of life," the view, namely, that the physical aspects of the world are the instruments of spiritual purpose. History on this view, is looked upon, not as a blind push of evolutionary mechanisms, but as a sacramental economy in which the hand of God never ceases to cause all things to work together for the accomplishment of his divine ends and goals. The "natural" is also divine, but it does not exclude divine action that transcends it, namely, the supernatural. The natural is but that part of the supernatural that, being repetitive and hence familiar, no longer excites surprise. The natural does, indeed, reveal God in his sovereign attributes, his "eternal power and Godhead." It does not, however, reveal his personal will and his redemptive purpose for mankind. Such knowledge requires a personal revelation. If there were no voices purporting to be the authentic "Thus saith the Lord" of a personal God, the religious life would lack the only object able to sustain it. It would be psychologically impossible to love a God "with all our heart, all our soul, all our mind" who remained forever veiled behind the impersonal phenomena of nature. Christianity stands for the conviction that the appearance of God on the plane of history is not only true in fact, but inevitable from the very nature of God. This view is pregnant with radical and revolutionary consequences. It makes the difference between "thick" and "thin" religion, to borrow an expression of William James's. It is the question of whether God makes very little difference, or whether he makes all the difference in the world. Christianity says that God makes all the difference in the world. Hence the Christian colleges, too, are pledged to the conviction that God makes all the difference in the world. And where God, the personal and living God, can thus be taken with the utmost seriousness, the attested supernatural aspects of Christianity no longer appear anomalous and incredible. Rather they appear "natural," and consistent with the character of God. Revelation, miracle, the incarnation of God in Christ, are not burdens laid on faith; nor are they some mythical projections of wishful thinking which have imposed themselves on our credulity. They are rather divine assurances that deliver us from the tyranny of soulless mechanism.

Christian truth has now, these thousands of years, withstood the searching tests of logical coherence and pragmatic success. We live in a rational world wherein truth, in the long run, is more persuasive than error. During all the centuries of the Christian era we have before us the testimony of countless witnesses who have found in a divine Christ a saving and cleansing power which brings that peace of God which passes all understanding. Unless we stand ready to believe that history is a chaos of moral irrationalities, we must reject the notion that the generations which brought forth all the moral sublimities of Christian history since Jesus Christ was crucified under Pontius Pilate, have founded their hopes upon a monstrous delusion and committed their souls to a blasphemous fraud. It is certainly pertinent to ask that pregnant question, "Do men gather grapes of thorns, and figs from thistles?"

We confront today on many sides, both within and without the church, the persistent demand that the high claims for a divine Christ be abandoned. The Christian Gospel is to be stripped of its supernatural features and reduced to the status of a humanitarian ethic. Or it is to be crushed beneath the juggernaut of a triumphant naturalism! In such circumstances those who know in whom they believe have a paramount duty to render an audible and decisive witness. The Christian college is one of the witnessing agencies of the church. She, like the church whose child she is, is dedicated to the great cause of the propogation of the Gospel and the extension of the kingdom of God. That is her chief value and her justification.

But if this be granted, we are faced with an apparent dilemma. Can the church college assume the responsibility of an agency witnessing to the purposes of God in Christ, without sacrificing its intellectual integrity? Is "witness" necessarily "propaganda" in the pejorative meaning of that term? Does such a role comport with that free and fearless search for truth which must mark any education worthy of the name? These questions must be faced, and I shall revert to them in the sequel.[3]

[3]They are involved in the question, "Is a Christian philosopher possible?" cf. Chapter VI.

Chapter IV

CULTURE, LIBERAL EDUCATION, AND THE HUMANITIES

We have spoken of the Christian college as the protagonist of Christian culture. In attempting to make explicit what is meant by Christian culture, we have brought together in the title of the present chapter three closely related concepts. One of these cannot be discussed without reference to the others. If culture is the end, then liberal education is the method, and the humanities are the chief means. But before further exploring the issues thus raised, it is necessary first to dispose of a number of banal and ludicrous misconceptions about that much-abused term "culture."

Some Misconceptions About Culture

Several generations ago, Matthew Arnold, in a celebrated volume of deft but devastating analysis called *Culture and Anarchy*, converted the word "culture" into a technical term in social criticism. Un-

48

fortunately, the term has since been so cheapened by being bandied about *ad nauseam* by its vulgar votaries that it has become difficult to use the term in respectable critical discussion

When we think of "culture," we are likely to recall the Thanatopsis Club in Sinclair Lewis' *Main Street,* in which the socialites of Gopher Prairie pursued the higher life with the aid of a club magazine called "Culture Hints." It appears, indeed, that the Thanatopsis Club's programs conveyed some hints of the subject. This year, as Mr. Lewis observes, "the Club was covering European literature." Next season it intended to "take up antique furniture and old china." At one session, we note, for example, "Gopher Prairie finished the poets." Mrs. Jenson read a brief paper on Shakespeare and Milton. Mrs. Warren followed with a few remarks on Byron, Scott, Moore, and Burns. Then Mrs. Mott gave ten minutes to Tennyson and Browning, followed by Mrs. Hick's concluding remarks on "other poets, including such persons as Coleridge, Wordsworth, Shelley, Gray, Mrs. Hemans, and Kipling." The program was triumphantly concluded with Ella Stowbody's dramatic recital of "The Recessional" and (by request) "An Old Sweetheart of Mine" as encore, accompanied by "Hearts and Flowers" on the piano.

Culture of the Gopher Prairie type evidently connotes a predilection for gush and effervescent puerilities. To others culture has meant a tortuous wrestling with the texts of dead languages, yielding perhaps a few odious odes of Horace and an ability to exclaim "O tempora, O mores!" To others, like the late Prof. Dewey, culture seems to connote the mild preoccupations of an effete "leisure class," or their late successors, the genteel middle classes. In either case Mr. Dewey suspected culture to be but an anachronism in our proletarian age.

The Meaning of Culture and of Liberal Education

Against these vapid ineptitudes and misconceptions might be set Arnold's original statement, that culture is simply "appreciative familiarity with the best that has been said and thought in the world." I prefer, however, to propound a more comprehensive definition. *By culture, as a normative ideal in education, I mean the comprehensive and harmonious maturing of human personality, through the development of man's intellectual, artistic, volitional, and spiritual capacities. Such a conception of culture is identical with the objective of liberal education,* and in this discussion these two terms might well be used interchangeably.

Perhaps it would be well to emphasize, however, the special significance of the term *liberal education* which, used substantively, is roughly synonymous with "culture." It is quite the same as what I have just defined as "cultural education," except that the term "liberal" places special emphasis on the state of inner and outer freedom, or the state of *liberation,* which ought to characterize a mature personality.

Historically and philosophically, of course, liberal education means the education appropriate to the ancient or medieval *liber* or freeman, as opposed to the education sufficient for slaves, serfs, and menials. But this association of liberal education with an aristocratic privileged class, though perhaps philologically justified, is, in terms of its modern meaning, only a historical accident. The permanent and essential meaning of the term liberal education (still today, let us note, the education appropriate to *free* men) *has to do with its liberating effect on human nature.*

The natural man without benefit of culture is in a state of bondage—a bondage from which he needs to be liberated. He is in bondage to ignorance, to irrational animal impulses, to esthetic and spiritual blindness. As such he needs to escape into the freedom of truth, of responsible choice, of esthetic and spiritual insight, and it is precisely liberal education that aims to do this. When a man possesses insight into the nature of himself and his world, when he intelligently directs his impulses toward rational ends, when he is voluntarily loyal to the basic values of truth, beauty, and goodness—only then does he come into possession of his full human inheritance.

All outward social and political freedom is dependent on this inner freedom of mind, esthetic sensibility, and conscience. Does not our Lord's pregnant saying, "Ye shall know the truth and the truth

shall make you *free"* suggest this comprehensive
ideal of liberal education, especially when we re-
member that the term "truth" does not mean intellectual information only, but is roughly equivalent
to the Old Testament conception of "wisdom," which
includes devotion to intellectual, moral, and religious
values?

Liberal Education's Program of Priorities

Let us, then enumerate the essential objectives of
true culture and of liberal education. Now, one general way in which this objective can be expressed
is this: Understanding the true ends of human life
properly precedes acquiring the means of livelihood.
The curse of our age is its *preoccupation with means*
and its *ignorance of ends.* We prostitute a stupendous
technical efficiency to childishly trivial and malicious
ends. Nothing in history is more ominous than the
spectacle of modern man, in so many respects still
a spiritual moron, strutting about brandishing an
atomic bomb. I am frank to voice my belief that
nothing but a truly liberal culture, based on Christian presuppositions and convictions, stands today
between man and ruin. That is the reason I am more
than ever impressed with the importance of Christian
liberal education, and the grave social responsibility
which rests upon the church colleges. Modern civilization must find purposes worthy of its great technical achievements, or perish.

This needed correlation of means and ends involves a series of pedagogical and ethical priorities: in the agent's character, in his insights, in his motives, in his ultimate loyalties.

The first is that *character is prior to conduct, that being must precede doing.*

A man's dependable conduct is the expression of his established character. One can be taught to *perform* the most desirable actions outwardly. But neither the blind force of social habit nor the threat of compulsion can give any guarantee that such desirable conduct will be dependably forthcoming, for neither fear nor expediency produces consistency. Only a virtuous character consecrated to true values can make a man dependable. For this reason a true culture must aim to foster that sensitivity to the spiritual values of life on which sound personal character is based. Thus liberal education insists on asking, "What manner of *man* are you to be?" Only first thereafter does it further inquire, "What ought you to *know* and what can you *do?*"

This leads to the second priority: The *appreciation of values take precedence over functional efficiency.*

Merely to teach men to parse nouns, dissect dogs, operate typewriters, assemble radios, or audit corporation accounts, with no insight into any worthy ends to which these desirable skills ought to be devoted for the enrichment of life, may merely contribute to the number of the world's clever scoundrels.

The defect of crass vocationalism in education is precisely this ignoring of all values (except cash values), and its exclusive concern with marketable skills. It consists largely in strictly utilitarian prescriptions for making money, by learning to ply a remunerative trade. The rapture of beauty, the joy of intellectual discovery, the mystery and tragedy of life, the wonder of nature, the dignity of noble living, the beauty of holiness—these things your practical Philistine cannot understand. Yet precisely in these experiences, through which the supremacy of mind and spirit stand revealed, does man discover the essential meaning of life, the life of "culture" which liberal education seeks to foster.

But values and ideals must not only be appreciated. There must be the positive will to pursue them and translate them into realities. This gives us a third priority: *Good motives must logically precede both passive insight and practical skill.*

It is not sufficient either to know the basic values of life or the means of implementing them if there be no motives dynamic enough to arouse action. Here, indeed, is a crux in education. How can strong motives for purposeful living be incited? This is a difficult question, too involved to linger on it here. I merely record my conviction that only as values are personalized and become the appropriate objects of personal affection, are we passionately moved to pursue them.

It is the great advantage of Christian education

that values are seen as the expression of the character and will of God. As men are inspired to love God, they find that all things true, lovely, and of good report, as aspects of the divine will, are embraced in this love. This reinforces the will's devotion to ideals by the immense power of personal affection. In any event the development of strong idealistic motivations and of effective good will is a fundamental aspect of true culture, and must, therefore, be included in the objectives of liberal education.

The final priority to which our general principle commits us is this: *Higher values precede lower ones.*

Higher values tend to be intrinsic, lower ones to be instrumental. Hence the latter are means to the former. The soul is more than the body, life is more than raiment. A man's highest good does not consist in the abundance of his possessions. A true culture rates the creation of the values of personal life, of intellect, of esthetic appreciation, of moral and religious devotion, as of greater value than the gratification of sensuous impulses on the animal level, or the empty pursuit of wealth and commercial success.

In endeavoring in this way to put first things first, liberal education seeks to deliver man from enslavement to his own immaturity. It thus seeks to place him in full possession of his humanity, that he might realize the true ends of his existence.

When all this has been conceded, it may be added that liberal education *does not ignore or disparage vocational efficiency.*

Men are called to work and to render efficient service in this world, and this necessity must not be despised. In a wider sense, liberal education both anticipates and prepares for vocation. Much subject matter is both vocationally functional and liberal in character and may thus fulfill both purposes at the same time. However, so fundamental does liberal education consider the antecedent liberal foundation for a vocation, that it must necessarily leave the detailed technical training necessary for most higher vocations to technical, trade, or professional schools, or to on-the-job training.

In these observations about "vocation," I have used the term in its conventional meaning, as synonymous with earning an economic livelihood. It should be said, however, that the term "vocation" or "calling" has a more fundamental and religious meaning. From the standpoint of Christianity, a man is called to the faithful discharge of *all* life's obligations.

Now, clearly, man is much more than a cog in the economic machine. No man is merely a bricklayer, a stenographer, a surgeon. He is a husband or a wife, a parent, a citizen, a good neighbor, a friend, a churchman, a reader of books, a patron of art and recreation, a club member, an amateur gardener, a fisherman. In all of these varied relationships he is called upon to apply whatever intelligence, proficiency, "good form," and moral excellence the occasion demands and his personal competence permits.

All these activities, organized into a harmonious pattern of life, constitute a man's vocation.

In this more fundamental and comprehensive sense, only liberal education, or culture, is genuinely vocational — far more "vocational" than the superficial utilitarianism that imagines man's economic functions alone to be important. This is one of the basic errors of Marxian materialism, with its economic interpretation of history and its overweening obsession with the problem of economic well-being. This error a true understanding of Christian culture must repudiate. It must insist, rather, that a man's vocation comprises the sum total of *all* life's obligations, not merely those involved in economic activity.

Three Criteria of Liberal Studies

Having considered what liberal studies are designed to do, we may now ask, What studies are liberal? In the light of the comprehensive character of culture that I have suggested, it appears that *no one study or group of studies can fulfill the liberal ideal by itself.*

Poetry without physics is perhaps no more liberal than mathematics without music. Man is a complex being and lives his total life in a complex of many relationships. Liberal education opposes all one-sidedness, narrowness, and distortion. It seeks to see life's issues in their true perspective, "to see life steadily and see it whole," as Arnold put it. Hence a variety of subjects must complement each other to secure this wholesome perspective.

In general, however, a subject is more liberal if it can meet three criteria. In the *first* place, *it must possess an intellectual content that addresses itself to man's analytical and theoretical capacities.* In this sense a course in algebra is liberal, while a course in barbering is not. *Secondly,* a subject, to be liberal, *must involve significant knowledge about man and his environment, natural and spiritual.* From this point of view, courses in biology and astronomy are liberal, while a course in spot-welding is not. *Finally, liberal studies increase man's appreciation of scientific, esthetic, moral, and religious values.* Hence poetry and history are more liberal than courses in office filing or potato culture.

These three criteria: intellectual content, human significance, and expressiveness of value, are, of course, relative, not absolute. Much depends upon how they are taught. A pedantic grad-grind can make a course in Plato illiberal, while a cultured scholar can discover liberal values in thermo-dynamics, or the anatomy of the cat. *No paper curriculum, no matter how well conceived, will make an alleged liberal arts college really liberal.* It is the personality of the teacher that counts toward this end.

A liberal arts college, to be genuinely a community of culture, must necessarily be composed of persons with keen intellectual interests, mature tastes, a passion for scholarly thoroughness, and some spiritual profundity. Without this it is a pretense and a sham, and the handsome, well-padded catalog and the plausible propaganda of the admissions office are but specious window-dressing. To recruit such cultured, Christian scholars to his faculty is the prime responsibility of a good college president (though, to succeed, his pecuniary sagacity must doubtless be not inferior to his idealism).

The Special Value of the Humanities

Though the point of view of the teacher is all-important, it still remains true, however, that certain subjects have by nature a special value for the purpose of liberal education. They are literature, art, history, philosophy, and religion—in short, the humanities.

If by liberal culture we mean the harmonious and comprehensive maturing of human personality through the development of man's intellectual, esthetic, moral, and spiritual capacities, it is obvious that the main burden of this program falls on the humanities. This is true because in these subjects the subjective life of man comes to its most passionate and creative expression. These subjects enshrine man's visions, his dreams, his supreme insights, his creative deeds, his understanding of the meaning and purposes of life.

Hence, granting the liberal possibilities of the natural and social sciences, they are still obviously defective as the principal constituent of an education that aims to be liberal. Their strict objectivity, their methodological exclusion of all value-judgments, cannot make them the adequate expression of man's convictions, or of his significant insights and appreciations. They report the impersonal facts *about* man or his world, but *they do not reveal his inner personal life,* that is, man himself. They load the mind with facts, but do not illuminate it with meaning, or inspire it to high purpose. In our day, which has witnessed the undesirable effects of an overemphasis on purely factual and scientific education, it is important to recognize anew the indispensable and time-honored primacy of the humanities in the ideal of liberal education.

I have spoken as if culture were primarily a matter of subject matter conveyed through formal classroom instruction. But much of its finer essence, the flower and perfection of it, is but the ripening effect of a subtle and silent influence of social environment, of the cultural community which a college ought properly to be.

Culture can only be contagiously transmitted within a living tradition, through the inspiration of vital personalities and the general tone and atmosphere of the entire academic community. This communal tone and atmosphere manifests itself variously in the intellectual keenness, the distinction of thought and expression, the elevation of taste, the catholicity of interest, the courtesy of deportment, that characterize the members of the academic community.

Even the outward beauty and dignity of the college campus and the excellence of its architecture and landscaping are significant as the external symbols for this inner spirit. A cheap and dingy physical plant is apt to be indicative of a similar impoverished spirit within. Hence physical attractiveness is an important aspect of the college as a cultural community. It silently moulds the mind and shapes the spirit in its own image and breeds a divine discontent with all that is misshapen, ugly, and deformed.

Thus the outcome of true culture corresponds to Wordsworth's definition of poetry. It is "the breath and finer spirit of all knowledge." This finer spirit which manifests itself in the unmistakable qualities of a cultured person—a poetic and sensitive mind, a lively and incisive intellectual enthusiasm, a passionate moral idealism, a sympathetic understanding of man, a life of humility and gratitude before God—this finer spirit, I say, cannot be taught; it must be "caught" by contagion. It is an intangible essence that radiates from persons.

Even though not every college teacher can be a great and shining light, a Kittredge of Harvard, a Gauss of Princeton, a Wenley of Michigan, it is quite possible for him to be a lesser luminary instead of an extinct satellite exuding merely a dull reflected glow.

CHAPTER V

THE PLACE OF NATURAL SCIENCE IN CHRISTIAN HIGHER EDUCATION

The question "What special interest does the Christian church have in sponsoring the study of natural science through its program of higher education?" has more than a merely casual significance.

The fact that the church-related colleges of this country have invested millions of dollars in buildings and laboratories for the teaching of science must certainly indicate a definite conviction that such instruction is a valuable, indeed an indispensable, part of their educational obligation. Perhaps, since I am not a scientist, I ought to justify my temerity in endeavoring to answer the question before us.

I venture to suggest that a scientific layman may

The substance of this chapter was given as an address at Capital University during a faculty conference in connection with the dedication of a new Science Hall, and was subsequently published in *Theology Today*, October, 1952.

quite properly be asked to explain the inclusion of natural science as a component part of a liberal and Christian program of higher education. For any such liberal and religious values, over and above the strictly professional utility of the study of science, ought to be intelligible to the average person without assuming more than a modest degree of technical comprehension.

It is from this non-professional point of view and in the hope of exhibiting these liberal values that I shall discuss the subject. In so doing, it will appear that the wholesome effects of including science in the program of Christian education are reciprocal. Science, as a dominant aspect of Western culture, has greatly profited from being sponsored under Christian auspices. On the other hand, Christian thought in general and theology in particular have been enriched and benefited by science, both by its new insights and by its methodology.

Christianity's Contribution to Science

A Christian who acknowledges his daily dependence on the grace of a beneficent Creator would certainly have the strongest and noblest motive for the study of nature. For nature is God's handiwork, and he who really loves God must be profoundly interested in all God's works and ways. God not only has given man the faculty of reason and has inspired him with the love of intellectual truth for its own sake, but in his creation God has given man—apart from his own ineffable Person—the grandest conceivable object of intellectual contemplation and an arena to test and to expand his powers of discovery. Clearly, for the Christian, the study of science may and should be an act of worship and adoration, a modern form of what the Psalmist called "delight in the law of the Lord."

The great truth that nature is God's handiwork inspires also another strong motive for scientific study. Since "the heavens are telling the glory of God and the firmament proclaims his handiwork," since "day to day pours forth speech, and night to night declares knowledge," since "his invisible nature, namely, his eternal power and deity, has been clearly perceived in the things that have been made," it is evident that creation is a very important work of God.

The Christian is obliged and is glad to hear *every* word that God speaks, and so he must necessarily listen to the word of God spoken in *creation*, as well as the word spoken in history by the prophets, and latterly, the word spoken by his Son, Jesus Christ. It is my contention that in the tremendous discoveries of modern science God has granted new insights to this generation which a faithful church must incorporate into her theology.

Such scientific discoveries have especially affected the cosmological and anthropological sections of dog-matics. Since, in God's world, all truth is his, and is one and self-consistent, it is necessary for any new truth so revealed to cast out any ancient errors or obsolete misconceptions. Willingness to do this is part of the Christian's pious obedience, which endeavors to bring every human thought captive to the word of God. For the word of truth *is* the Word of God—wherever it may be found.

Science, then, has its own testimony to bring to the validity of faith regarding the being and nature of God. This alone would be a sufficient reason for its inclusion in a Christian program of education.

One of the effects of Barthian influence on modern Christian thought is to disparage, if not to dismiss, the knowledge of God mediated by nature. In the interest of an alleged exclusively Christo-centric self-disclosure of God, the clear force of Romans 1:20; Psalm 19; Psalm 104; Acts 14:17, etc., is deviously evaded, or exegetically toned down. All that these strictures show, however, is that the "theistic arguments" are religiously *insufficient*, not that they are *invalid*. As Paul Althaus says, "Nature prevents one from being an atheist. But it presents no unambiguous image of the living will which acts therein, and therefore does not make possible a definite personal relationship to God."[1]

Nevertheless, Althaus conclusively defends their

---

[1]Paul Althaus, *Die christliche Wahrheit*, I, p. 107, C. Bertelsmann, Gutersloh, 1947.

validity, if not their sufficiency. "The attempt to
limit God's self-disclosure," he says, "to the I-thou
situation, the existential encounter, is not theologi-
cally tenable. It is no more than a prejudice that
must be finally abandoned. . . . Theology dare not be
indifferent to the fact that Epistemology, Metaphysics, Physics, and Biology find themselves confronted
with the question concerning God and under the necessity of formulating the theistic concept. For God is
one, and, in the final analysis, knowledge is a unity.
All tidings of God belong together and demand a
synoptic consideration. In so far as theology takes
God's self-certification in scientific reflection seriously, she acknowledges the profound unity of human knowledge and promotes the consciousness of
the ultimate unity of the sciences. This is part of
theology's responsibility toward our total cultural
life."[2]

Considering these motives for the study of science
—which also entail the very important consequence
of reverence for the genius of reason as a divinely
given faculty—it is not surprising to observe that
what is called "modern science" is in reality a peculiar product of the Christian world.

In making this claim I do not overlook the indispensable preparatory work of the Greeks in pro-
pounding philosophical problems and in pioneering
the techniques of logic, analysis, and general mathematics. Also I do not wish to underrate the influence

----

[2]*Ibid.*, pp. 92-93.

of Stoicism and the Roman conception of law as a *cosmic* as well as a juristic system of relationships. As Whitehead says, "All this was excellent . . . but it was not science as we understand it."[3]

Three things were lacking which awaited the coming of Christianity before systematic science could be developed. Two of these were contributed by Christian theism in general; the third was a by-product of the spirit of the Reformation.

First of all, ethical monotheism, and ethical monotheism alone, implied the necessary axioms presupposed by the scientific method and expressed in the faith of the scientific practitioner. These axioms are: the unity of the world, the uniformity of the world, and the rationality of the world. All three aspects are corollaries of the theistic conception of a God of personal intelligence, who constitutes a single, universal, and intelligible world ground.

The principle of the rationality of the world is expressed in the Johannine doctrine that the world is the creation of the divine Logos. The term "logos," in this context, does not lose its Greek meaning, namely, the rational principle of divine self-manifestation, but acquires a Christian enrichment. So understood, it provides a firm basis for the confidence of science that the world is amenable to human investigation and that the intelligibility of nature is the objective counterpart of the laws of human reason. A disciplined rationalism is, there-

---

[3]*Science and the Modern World* (Mentor Books Edition), p. 8.

fore, within bounds, a necessary condition for the development of science.

Precisely, this was supplied by Christian theology.

To quote again from Whitehead in *Science and the Modern World:* "It needs but a sentence to point out how the habit of definite exact thought was implanted in the European mind by the long dominance of scholastic logic and scholastic divinity. The habit remained after the philosophy had been repudiated, the priceless habit of looking for an exact point and of sticking to it when found. . . . The Middle Ages formed one long training of the intellect of Western Europe in the sense of order."[4]

A second factor that made science a peculiar product of the Christian world was the esthetic nature-mysticism that inspires man to approach nature with intense enthusiasm and with passionate attachment. The "love of nature" that "holds communion with her visible forms" is a religious sentiment, specifically a Christian sentiment. I have already explained how this attitude necessarily grows out of the belief in God as the Creator. Greek, Chinese, and Indian thought never attained the clear and serene convictions of monotheistic religion.

Nature, therefore, for these civilizations—far from being the manifestation of supreme order, wisdom, and goodness—was, on the contrary, the theater of

[4]*Science and the Modern World* (Mentor Books Edition), pp. 12-13.

inscrutable, and dangerous, forces. At best she was disparaged as "illusion." In either case nature was approached with cautious circumspection. As a consequence, no real nature lovers were ever produced by these otherwise sophisticated cultures. Christian culture alone inspired men to approach the study of nature with devotion and with the eager confidence that she would reward her devotees with a vision of divine wisdom and glory, and would prove beneficent if her laws were faithfully obeyed.

I have alluded to a third influence, which made science a product of the Christian world, which was, however, more specifically the manifestation of the Protestant spirit.

The history of science will show that the greatest contributions to scientific progress have been made, with some important exceptions, since the Renaissance, and mostly by a few Catholic "heretics" and a large company of Protestant scholars.

Catholicism in the past as well as in the present has proved, on the whole, an infertile ground for the growth of science because of its restrictions on freedom of thought and its inquisitorial suppression of any truth that happened to challenge its dogmatic tradition. Protestantism, despite an occasional lapse, repudiated these obstructions to scientific progress because they were morally repugnant to the spirit of free inquiry and of honest religion. Moreover, in its distinctive doctrine of justification, Protestantism provided the theological basis for the attitude of humility before the acts of God and for the *receptive, rather than the prescriptive* function of reason.[5]

These religious motives are congenial to the attitude of empiricism and the experimental method. This is the method of inductive science as opposed to rationalism and the prescriptive use of reason. A careful consideration of the structure of the sciences will show that the systematic coherence of these systems is only the logical consequence of certain primary truths, which themselves are inexplicable and rest solely upon the contemplation of brute facts.

These primary facts of nature are not known to us as necessary truths, like the axioms of geometry or logic. They are not self-evident to our reason; they are facts which must be accepted without either logical or teleological insight. The constant of gravity, the charge of the electron, the velocity of light, the value of Plank's constant, the quantum theory, the elementary atomic particles, the metabolic peculiarities of animal and vegetable life, the proliferation of biological species—these facts and countless others cannot be rationally *understood;* they can only be accepted with natural piety.

---

[5]This might seem to contradict our justifying a "pious rationalism" on the basis of the logos doctrine. The answer is that a limited rationalism and empiricism are complementary processes. Nature's primary forms of order (laws, formulas, etc.) are empirically *discovered,* and have no demonstrable a priori necessity. *Once known,* they furnish the universals necessary for systematic deduction.

All attempts, such as Hegel's, to exhibit in these facts a transparent logical necessity have proved abortive. Nature turns out to be more astounding than the mind of man could have imagined. She constantly confronts reason with unpredictable surprises. Truth is indeed stranger than fiction. In empirical science man has been forced to admit: "My thoughts are not your thoughts, neither are my ways your ways, says the Lord." Prof. Whitehead, speaking of the church's opposition to the discoveries of Galileo, correctly observes that "it is a great mistake to conceive this historical revolt [of the empirical scientists] as an appeal to reason. On the contrary, it was through and through an anti-intellectualist movement. . . . It was based on a recoil from the inflexible rationalism of medieval thought."[6]

In this new attitude of humility before the fact, in the renunciation of the pride of rational insight into the creative mind of God, we have the intellectual analogue of the religious relation of man to God expressed in the doctrine of justification, wherein, similarly, man cannot prescribe to God his duty on the basis of any principles of justice and desert, but must humbly wait on the inexplicable grace of God.

In noting that Christian theism in general, and Protestant religious culture in particular, nurtured the post-Renaissance scientific movement, we see the historical justification for the fundamental interest which the church college should take in scientific

---

[6]*Ibid.*, p. 9.

study. *This interest is neither accidental nor dictated by expediency, but an essential, though historically delayed, expression of Christian culture and its theological world view.*

It is significant, I believe, to discover that the first modern university to adopt the Copernican worldview officially as part of its curriculum was Wittenberg. Despite Luther's diatribes against Copernicus, as reported in the *Table-Talks*, he did not intervene to prevent Melanchthon's protégé, Dr. Rhaeticus, Professor of Mathematics, from introducing the new astronomy, though it was widely denounced as in conflict with the cosmology of the Scriptures. Dr. Rhaeticus brought out on the press of Hans Lufft of Nuremberg—Luther's own publisher and the printer of the German Bible—the first complete edition of the works of Copernicus. The editorial notes and introduction to this edition were written by Luther's associate, Dr. Andreas Osiander.

The example of Wittenberg was soon followed by all the Protestant universities of Germany. Thus was prepared that preeminence which for three centuries the German universities enjoyed as the home of systematic scholarship and the vanguard of scientific progress. In taking an interest in scientific studies the Christian colleges may well aspire to be worthy heirs to a notable tradition.[7]

---

[7]Cf. Werner Elert, *Morphologie des Luthertums,* pp. 369 ff. (I. 15). Concerning the later objection to Copernicus by dogmaticians like Calov and Hutter, Elert comments, "Thus, the Bible, which

Another Christian motive, which led church-sponsored education to take a strong interest in scientific studies, should be mentioned. Applied science is obviously an instrument of good will and an effective means for the propagation of the Gospel. It has contributed much to the relief of distress, the alleviation of want, the cure of disease, and the service rendered by hospitals, clinics, and asylums. The message of the gospel is speeded on its way by the printing press, by rapid transport and communication, by radio and television. Our missionaries have found the airplane of great service in reaching remote and inaccessible locations on the mission field. The same science that too often magnifies the power of greed, lust, violence, and pride may augment the beneficence of justice, sympathy, and neighborly love. If the church can use science in its service, it seems fitting that the church should help to promote scientific truth itself, as well as the good will to use science for righteous ends.

Finally, it may reasonably be claimed that the promotion of science under Christian auspices contributes to scientific progress itself by saving science from the excesses of its own votaries.

The modern superstition called "scientism" is a case in point. This "ism" holds that science has estab-

---

Luther read as law and gospel, was converted into a scientific canon. But this retrogression from the evangelical standpoint came too late to call in question the great contribution which the Reformation made to the development of the natural sciences" (p. 377).

lished a materialistic or a naturalistic metaphysics according to which all reality is ultimately describable in terms of physics and mechanical causality. This metaphysics denies the reality of spirit, freedom, teleology, God, and the supernatural. For it, duty is an illusion somehow generated by atomic friction, while values are, at best, only another name for organic desires. They are held to be entirely without cosmic significance or support. The only valid knowledge is said to be obtainable by what is called the "scientific method" — which is limited to physical sense-perception, experiment, and quantitative measurements.

Naturalism has committed many sins in the name of science. It is a form of scientific obscurantism, which has been effectively discredited by the advance of science itself, but largely under the leadership of those scientists whose theistic persuasions, based on Christian experience, have freed their minds from the hypnotic influence of materialistic assumptions and enabled them to see the evidence of spirit and intelligence at work in the universe. Not a few of these eminent scientists are the product of Christian colleges and universities. A healthy and enlightened Christianity, as the plight of Russia shows, is indispensable for keeping science itself truly objective and preventing its degeneration into naturalistic superstition.

Thus far I have been discussing the various ways in which Christian culture, in accordance with its own genius, has nurtured the scientific movement. I have tried to show that interest in the propagation of the study of creation—or systematic natural science—is, therefore, no mere concession to foreign or secular interests, but a natural and logical manifestation of the church's faith. Paraphrasing a saying of Terrence, the Christian must say, "I am a Christian, and nothing that concerns the Divine is foreign to me."

Science's Contribution to Christianity

Let us now reverse our point of view and ask, conversely, what the study of science has to contribute to the faith and practices of the church.

It will perhaps be obnoxious to some, especially those of Barthian persuasion, to be told that they have anything to learn from non-biblical sources. We are, of course, dependent on the Bible for our knowledge of God as the sovereign Creator, as the one who demands righteousness, and especially as the Father whose redemptive love is manifested in Christ and salvation. Science adds nothing to soteriology. But science has greatly widened our horizons in matters of cosmology, biology, and anthropology, subjects which necessarily occupy a prominent position in theology.

Historical science and archeology have also put ancient history in better perspective. This, combined with the science of source criticism, has provided

modern scholars with a basis for the historical interpretation of ancient documents, including the
documents of the Bible, which greatly improves our
understanding and appreciation of the scriptural
record of revelation. In discovering how God's abso-
lutes emerge progressively out of the relativities of
history, we are in less danger than previous generations of Christian thinkers of imputing the human,
which always means the finite and the defective,
to God.

One important contribution which science makes
to an understanding of Christianity is helping to
shatter man's invincible egoism and anthropocentric
bias.

The Copernican revolution was a resounding
scientific blow to man's self-esteem. It coincided
historically with the return by the Reformation from
a man-centered to a God-centered theology, that is,
from a religion of human work-righteousness to a
religion of divine grace. The advance of science has
only deepened this impression for thoughtful minds.
Man today confronts a stupendous universe that
seems to have no detectable human relevance. It
contains fantastic forms and forces that completely
repel human sentiment and comprehension.

Nature in her domesticated aspects may be senti-
mentally charming but, taken as a whole, she is awe-
some and terrifying. Obviously, then, the universe
is *not* tailored to man's measure. Its illimitable vast-
ness in time and space is both a measure of God's

eternity and man's creaturely insignificance. Its apparent appalling indifference to man and all his works burdens the sensitive mind with a sense of desolation and dereliction. "What is man that thou art mindful of him?"—unless, indeed, some assurance can be found that the terrible God of nature is also to be trusted!

But even so, science reminds us that the sublime God of the galaxies will not consent to be reduced by us to petty parochial formulas. As the Book of Job teaches, the God revealed in nature is a stern warning against all anthropomorphic puerilities, all petty gods created in our own image. It is not only Milton who, in *Paradise Lost*, has tended to represent God as a somewhat narrow-minded Puritan divine. Orthodoxies have been prone to impute many childish trivialities to God.

Whoever would persuade the enlightened mind today, however, must preach a God worthy of the sublime Being revealed in nature, from the atoms to the spiral nebulae.

It cannot be too strongly emphasized that no form of Christianity can hope to win the adherence of the future unless its theology is consistent with the established facts of natural and historical science. If Christianity is true, then no scientific discovery can invalidate the established and objective data of Christian faith. Where theological conclusions conflict with the *established* facts of science, the former must inevitably be revised or discarded. Fundamen-

talist attitudes which seek to commend Christianity
by browbeating science, by substituting amateur
scientific vagaries for the accredited conclusions of
the experts, or by mistaking primitive, poetical, or
literary thought forms for scientific literalism, are not
only obsolete but do untold harm by encouraging
honest minds to shun facts.

There is no greater sin committed against young
minds than to force them into the false dilemma of
having to choose between Christian faith and mental honesty. No faith is tenable at the cost of strict
intellectual integrity. Christianity is nothing if not
ruthlessly honest.

It is, therefore, the duty of the Christian college
to interpret the facts of Christianity to the present
generation of eager truth-seekers in a way consistent
with the whole body of modern knowledge. Only so
will the church of Christ win the support of the best
minds of our day and be able to reestablish in the
modern world that respect and authority which she
once enjoyed.

Religious thinkers, like other scholars, must never
cease to cultivate a more conscientious observance
of the intellectual virtues—an observance to which
science owes much of its success. These virtues are:
humility before the fact, receptiveness to new truth,
vigilance against dogmatic preconceptions, willingness to abandon obsolete ideas, thoroughness and
comprehensiveness in analysis and research, tolerance of divergent views so far as such differences

result from different estimates of inconclusive evidence.

It is an astounding anomaly that theological disputants have so often in the past praised and practiced every virtue except strict intellectual honesty. The history of doctrinal controversy is marred by pride, obscurantism, dogmatic prepossession, intolerance, and the illusions of infallibility. It is true that these defects have also blighted much scientific and philosophical thought. But one has a right to expect the servants of God by the very nature of their profession to set the best example of intellectual integrity.

Denominational divisiveness and the mutual intolerance that has commonly been practiced by all branches of Christendom would be largely mitigated if controversialists could be induced to apply to religious discussion the elementary techniques in common use among men of science.

These techniques are by no means infallible, but they provide the best safeguard thus far available against erroneous thinking. I seriously suggest that the adoption of such a method of thinking would do more to further the ecumenical search for the lost unity of Christendom than any other single measure that could be adopted. To doubt it is to doubt the persuasive power of truth and the willingness of the Holy Spirit to lead men into the truth they earnestly search for.

Included in such a procedure are four basic ideals

of scientific thought which I single out for special emphasis. I assume, of course, that all parties agree on the moral obligation to seek and respect truth, on the logical canons of valid thinking, and on the duty to respect freedom of thought and discussion as the indispensable prerequisite to honest thinking and as the means of detecting and eliminating error. This being assumed, what principles of the scientific method are applicable to theological discussion?

The first of these is the determination to rise above personal and corporate subjectivism by cultivating an *objective point of view.*

This is not what has sometimes been derided as "voraussetzungslose Wissenschaft," or the endeavor to think without presuppositions or antecedent convictions. This is impossible, as elementary epistemology shows. But it does mean (1) that we are aware of our presuppositions, (2) that we hold them as grounded on evidence that can produce rational conviction, rather than on such emotions as self-conceit or pride of tradition, (3) that we entertain our presuppositions critically, not dogmatically, and, therefore, subject to revision on the evidence of new insights.

There are two attitudes, especially, that must be sacrificed to this scientific striving for genuine objectivity. One is pride in the exclusive "purity" of our own religious tradition. It is possible to cherish the great values of one's religious heritage without making unfounded monopolistic claims. The other is the illusion of infallibility, which prevents adopting an open and receptive attitude toward those of different persuasions.

The second aspect of scientific method which is applicable to religious discussion is the technique of *collective thinking* by men who mutually respect each other, are genuinely anxious to understand one another, and who are receptive to new truth wherever it may be found.

Need we be reminded today of the futility of firing long-distance artillery shells of controversy over political iron curtains? Well, the same applies to firing them across denominationally fortified walls. This method is slow at best, and usually productive of polemical arrogance and special pleading. It abounds in arbitrary assertions and uncontradicted assumptions. Face-to-face discussion, on the other hand, under conditions which engender mutual respect for opposing opinions is much more apt to discover the direction in which mutual agreement may be found. Second only in value to such face-to-face discussion is the free professional journal, in which men of different views may discuss and challenge each other's conclusions. Wherever these methods have been adopted by churchmen, there has resulted an evident trend toward greater unity.

Thirdly, it is necessary to *analyze* divergent convictions so as to isolate the exact points or difference between them. Such analysis will make clear precisely on what matters there is agreement and on

what there is disagreement. No discussion need be
wasted on matters on which opponents already agree.
When the precise points of disagreement have been
clearly defined, it is possible to examine the available evidence on which such points of divergence
are accepted by men of different beliefs. Clearly,
such evidence ought to be forthcoming and be capable of being presented for rational examination.
If this were done with honesty and thoroughness,
conclusions would soon be possible regarding the
validity and convincing character of such evidence
to other reasonable minds. If part of this evidence—
as is quite likely in the sphere of religious faith—is
not so much factual and logical, but in the realms
of moral and spiritual appreciation of values, this too
can be discovered and its significance more readily
assessed.

Finally, it is an essential aspect of scientific thought
to grant divergence of opinion without fear of professional excommunication. *Tolerance is the necessary
consequence of abandoning the pretensions of infallibility.*

This attitude is really an honest acceptance of the
limitations imposed on any individual thinker by the
Creator. We are tolerant, not because we are indifferent about truth, but because we are so concerned
about it that we desire to be delivered from our own
deficiencies and errors. Men may indeed be rightly
certain about some basic "fact," but vague and naive
in the conceptual understanding thereof. God has

chosen to make men different, subject to different environments, histories, cultures, and individual experiences.

This absolutely defeats any mere uniformity of thought, and perhaps with good reason. For it is alike an incentive to individual responsibility in thought and belief, and to a ceaseless quest after the larger truth. Now, the church sadly needs to learn and to apply this principle. Some form of fundamental creedal subscription is, doubtless, a necessary prerequisite to any genuine cooperation among Christians in worship, thought, and action.

But the longer I reflect on the matter, the more firmly I am persuaded that within this larger unity of the faith a generous latitude of opinion is the only view consistent with the rights and dignity of human nature. If it be said that such a view means the blurring of confessional and denominational convictions, this is not necessarily the case. To be sure, mutual intolerance and non-recognition of a common Christian fellowship would disappear. But surely this would be no loss! Confessional differences would remain and be respected so long as the evidence for such views supports only problematic conclusions.

Such differences, it seems, are largely the unavoidable expression of that variety in human nature which it has pleased God to impose upon us. It might, of course, be said that confessional differences also indicate different degrees of responsiveness to the enlightenment of the Spirit. But this claim dare be made only with great humility and with fear and trembling. Theological differences would, then, be the manifestation of a certain amount of *variety within the unity* of the Christian brotherhood.

But such divergencies of honest thought, like the same phenomena in the field of science, would not, however, be a basis for excommunication and non-recognition. They would, instead, constitute a standing invitation *within the fellowship* to a persistent and patient search for the common truth. Thus, in time, this application of the principle of tolerance for divergent opinion would heal the breaches of Christendom without encouraging indifferentism and the sacrifice of honest convictions.[8]

If religious thinkers could learn lessons such as these from the illustrious example set by scientists, it would in itself justify the interest the church has in promoting the study of science in its schools and colleges. By impressing the ideals of scientific and scholarly thought and procedure upon the minds of college graduates, especially upon the church's future leaders and theologians, the teaching of science would make a valuable contribution to the cause of Christian unity. Here, too, the church's wisdom in fostering science "would be justified of her children."

---

[8]The avoidance of this indifferentism to truth—a sin unfortunately called "unionism" — by no means, therefore, necessitates denominational isolationism. The scientist shows us how to practice tolerance with conviction and integrity.

CHAPTER VI

THE PLACE OF PHILOSOPHY
IN
CHRISTIAN HIGHER EDUCATION

In considering the problems of Christian higher education, I hope it may be thought no undue display of professional egotism to discuss the status of philosophy, since—unlike calculus or European history—philosophy, among the orthodox, stands under the shadow of suspicion.

To the layman the word "philosophy" often suggests something tricky and formidable, while to the earnest Christian, mindful of St. Paul's warning to the Colossians to beware of "philosophy and empty deceit," it not infrequently implies rather the devil's snare than a word of wisdom. But the essential idea of philosophy is simple, and, so understood, the possession of a "philosophy" proves to be inevitable.

Your philosophy is essentially your view about the ultimate nature of the world and man and about the meaning and value of human existence. The Christian who believes that this is God's world, that we are his creatures, and that man's highest felicity is to "love God and enjoy him forever" has a philosophy, a world-view. Technically, this view, when fully elaborated, would be called Christian theism.

The term "world-view"—the German *Weltanschauung* — indicates philosophy's ultimate concern: the attainment of a comprehensive understanding of the nature of the universe and man's place therein, for the purpose of shedding light on the mystery of existence and the meaning and purpose of human life.

In searching for answers to such ultimate questions, philosophy joins hands with religion in a common enterprise. It is clear that insofar as philosophy seeks to interpret the nature of the world as described by the scientist and the historian, inquiring into the world's meaning, purpose, and value, philosophy transcends purely factual inquiry by virtue of the inclusion of ethical, esthetic, and spiritual issues. These issues are the major concern of the arts and the humanities. In philosophy, then, the world of science and the world of the humanities confront each other in an intellectual summit meeting to establish a cultural *entente* mutually agreeable to both.

The Objectives and Attitudes of Philosophy

What, then, are the objectives and attitudes that the teacher of philosophy seeks to encourage among his students? Some of them are identical with the ideals of the scientific method in general. I would name *intellectual objectivity* first.

By this is *not* meant the endeavor to think without presuppositions, cultivating a so-called *voraussetzungslose Wissenschaft*. By objectivity I mean rather an open-minded receptivity to new truth, a self-effacing humility before the fact, a renunciation of that dogmatic subjectivism that identifies final truth with the beliefs acquired by uncritical conformity to the social environment. True, after critical examination, a traditional belief may well be vindicated, but we must not—out of respect for intellectual honesty — merely unconsciously assume its validity. While, therefore, one cannot think without making assumptions, the trained thinker, on the one hand, knows what assumptions he is making, and, on the other hand, is prepared, having critically evaluated them, to justify their validity.

In addition to the attitude of intellectual objectivity, philosophy seeks to inculcate a dependable *intellectual methodology.*

Such a method includes the usual procedures of the scholarly mind. It includes willingness to entertain a methodological doubt pending critical re-evaluation of a belief or theory. It includes also striving for clarity and adequacy of definition, and utilizing the widest possible range of established facts that are relevant to the solution of a problem. It includes the method of intellectual experimentation by means of rigorous logical analysis, testing hypotheses by their ability to illuminate and rationalize a wide range of human experience. Philosophy presents such material eminently suited to the practice of such scholarly procedure.

Again, the successful pursuit of philosophy demands *intellectual breadth*.

It is obvious that the attainment of a total world-view must allow the totality of human knowledge and experience to present its testimony. Philosophy must give due consideration to values as well as facts, to art as well as science, to history as well as nature, to the spiritual as well as the material, and to the existentially personal as well as the conceptually-grasped impersonal. The pursuit of philosophy therefore requires a broad culture and a catholicity of interests.

Of course, no philosopher—being but human and finite—can literally "take all knowledge for his province." But while he must renounce much minutia, he must necessarily aspire to understand the broad generalities of different areas of knowledge. He should know the major features of the scientific world-picture, the main patterns of man's history and culture, and he should have personal acquaintance with the pervasive features of man's moral, artistic, and religious experience.

In striving for such breadth, philosophy runs the danger of becoming superficial by spreading itself too thin. A philosopher is in danger of being a jackof-all-trades and master of none. But though this danger exists, it must nevertheless be faced as inherent in the nature of the philosophic task. However, out of deference to the virtues of extreme specialism, the philosopher—though he is the "generalist" *par excellence*—still strives to allay his scholarly conscience by at least "knowing one thing well."

But encyclopedic breadth alone tends to be shallow. Another philosophic virtue is *intellectual depth*.

This is hard to define. It does not consist in the flaunting of obscure jargon and of a lot of formidable $64 polysyllables derived from Greek and Latin. Novices are often tempted to produce in this manner an illusion of profundity, whereas some of the deepest thinkers write simply and lucidly.

True depth, on the contrary, stems from a deep sympathy with human life, a sensitive personal appreciation of its ultimate issues, its supernal heights, as well as its tragic depths. These dimensions appear only when man learns to view his finitude and mortality against the immensities of his cosmic background and seeks to understand the precariousness of his existence in the light of his moral, esthetic, social, and religious experience.

But of such breadth and depth comes philosophy's ultimate objective, *an intellectual and existential conviction* concerning the meaning and purpose of the world and man.

It is this outcome that justifies the proud term "philosophy," with etymologically means "love of wisdom." Wisdom must be distinguished from mere knowledge. The latter includes both factual information and its derivative, technical know-how. Wisdom, on the other hand, subordinates information and technology to the genuinely worth-while objectives of human life. Its philosophic vision claims an understanding of the true values attainable by human life and harnesses human energy and purpose to their attainment.

Wisdom, therefore, makes technology the servant of spiritual purpose. It sees that knowledge and technology are largely means to ends, justified only by the values they help to create. The Christian's philosophic vision sees the world as divine, directed to accomplish the creative purposes of God. It sees that the highest human values are attained only when man realizes the divine purpose of his existence by directing his purpose to the fulfillment of God's will.

In seeking to lead the student of philosophy to the attainment of these objectives, intellectual objectivity, intellectual methodology, intellectual breadth, intellectual depth, and intellectual conviction, the teacher of philosophy must observe procedures consistent with such goals. His means must not frustrate his ends. He must himself be objective, employ scholarly procedure, and manifest a certain amount of breadth, depth, and wisdom.

One of the initial problems of the college teacher

of philosophy is that his students rarely have any formal acquaintance with the subject.

Philosophy is not studied in high school, at least not formally under that name. Hence the teacher of philosophy cannot assume a previously acquired interest in the subject. He must therefore whet the appetite of the student to strange fare and incite his interest to explore some largely unknown territory. If the teacher is a dull pedant, a dry retailer of abstract theories and speculations, lacking in wit, imagination, and vivacity—then, alas, he has already lost the battle.

Here, perhaps more than in most subjects, the personality of the teacher is of great importance. The teacher must be able to impart to the student the excitement of adventurous thought, the exhilaration of large and generous vision, and the vital stimulation imparted by contact with a mind that exudes enthusiasm and manifests some originality and penetration.

I have probably described the ideal college professor in general, not merely the professor of philosophy. Still it is true, I believe, that in those fields where value appreciations are involved, such as the humanistic disciplines, the personality of the teacher tends to count for relatively more than the intrinsic importance of the subject matter.

Again, the teacher of philosophy is perhaps more prone than others to encounter the current Philistinism that doubts the value of any study that cannot be translated into cash value. "Philosophy bakes no bread," it is said; though this should be no disparagement, since a great Teacher has said, "Man shall not live by bread alone."

Philosophy shares this common disparagement with literature and the arts. "I have no practical use for this, so why waste my time studying it?" is a familiar student refrain. This vulgar illusion results from failure to see the difference between living a life and making a living. This illusion is particularly strong in our country. Man's felicity, we tend to believe, consists in attaining the "American Standard of Living."

This often means little more than surfeiting man with food, clothing, fun, and technical gadgets, while he remains spiritually and inwardly mean, shallow, mediocre, and subject to neurotic instability. But philosophy, art, and religion exist precisely to dispel this illusion of the obtuse Philistine. The teachers of these subjects, therefore, must radiate a certain amount of evangelistic unction which is capable of converting the culturally blind and obtuse to a new vision of life. This unction is the aura of a dynamic personality, not the attribute of subject matter.

There are several attitudes towards his students which the philosopher must observe due to the nature of his subject. He must, for example, encourage students to treat the various theories and schools of philosophy with the respect their measure of truth deserves.

The philosopher, while of course he has his own convictions, must eschew fanatical partisanship or mere intellectual propaganda, in the debased meaning of that term. It is axiomatic in philosophy that no theory, however generally defective it has proved to be, has commanded the allegiance of large numbers of men without some measure of truth which accounted for its power to win support.

Thus no influential doctrine is wholly false; its errors, meanwhile, often serve to illuminate the greater truth. Materialism, for example, is the metaphysical antithesis of theism; yet materialism has a measure of truth that justifies a protest against a false, sentimental, and complacent spirituality.

Communism is the opposite of a free-enterprise economy, but it would be a grave mistake to neglect the justifiable rebuke that Communism presents to a socially irresponsible Capitalism obsessed with the supreme importance of making money. These examples show that one must study any system or theory with enough respect and patience to understand the element of truth in it that commended such a view to some great mind and his many followers.

By the same token, it is necessary in teaching philosophy to respect the opinions of the student.

Such opinions are not infrequently naive and ill formed. Nevertheless, it would be an error to reject or ridicule such immature views. First, it is encouraging to see the student doing his own thinking. Secondly, his views probably contain some measure of truth. Thirdly, this degree of insight which he already has is the teacher's opportunity to suggest that some additional facts might correct his perspective or warrant alternative points of view.

When all is said and done, however, there are a large number of questions in philosophy for which no final or definitive answers are possible. One can frequently defend only the hypothesis that seems most probable, that according to one's measure of insight seems most concordant with known facts, valid value-judgments, and the general trend of human experience. In philosophy, Bishop Butler's dictum that "probability is the guide of life" is preeminently true.

Belief in philosophy involves a certain extrapolation beyond the demonstrable facts. It is thus the analogue of faith in the sphere of religion. Thus the student must learn that in this life we are required to live with less than demonstrable certainty, that we must stake our life's ventures, not on absolute guarantees, but on "the soul's invincible surmise." To describe existence is by no means to understand it. Philosophy reminds us that, surrounded as we are by ultimate mystery, fanatical dogmatism is, more often than not, no more than the conceit of the ignorant, which betokens, not simply ignorance, but, what is even worse, ignorance of one's ignorance.

Philosophy in the Church College

One of the problems that confront a philosopher in a church college is the student who arrives well indoctrinated by his pastor in a species of narrow biblical fundamentalism.

This student is convinced that Christians must still fight evolutionists, that the world was made in six solar days of twenty-four hours each, and that God spoke Hebrew when he said, "Let there be light." Now, it is highly probable that none of these assertions, taken in their obvious meaning, are true, and that none of them are essential to the historic Christian faith. Nonetheless, it would be a mistake to dissuade such a student of his errors rudely by a purely negative and destructive approach. After all, such statements express a vital belief in God's reality and the reality of God's creative and redemptive activity in cosmic and in human history.

Here one must heed the injunction not to uproot the wheat with the tares. One must never tear down without offering something constructive in its place. With a little patience the student may be led to see, with no violent or excessive jolt to his faith, that while we must indeed confute the evolutionary *materialist*, evolution as such may well be only a divine *method* of creation; that the succession of creative days of the Genesis story symbolizes the progressive and orderly stages of creation in cosmic time; that the reiterated and majestic juxtaposition of the words "Let there be" and "There was" expresses sublimely the irresistible power and the rational purpose of the Creator who calls worlds out of nothingness in response to his will and his wisdom. After a while the student comes to see that in a divine world, ordained and sustained by the Creator, the reference of events to secondary causes and natural laws does not exclude divine agency, but merely illuminates the divine method.

Like Socrates, the modern teacher of philosophy is often suspected of being a corrupter of youth. Among his protégés will be a few who "catch on," acquire a taste for independent thinking, and discover that they cannot remain uncritical conformists within the pattern of an inherited tradition.

Strange to say, there are some teachers who resent this loss of the student's intellectual docility and the attitude of passive acquiescence in familiar clichés and well-worn institutional stereotypes. Such audacity of dissent is thereupon attributed to the sinful pride which results from being corrupted by philosophy. The worst is the case of the student who has casually contemplated the ministry as a vocation, but who in consequence of studying philosophy changes his mind and decides to pursue his new interest in graduate school instead of entering the theological seminary. When this occurs the philosopher must sustain the opprobrium of being a pernicious enemy of the church bent on overthrowing the kingdom of God.

For my part, I vigorously reject the imputation. I rejoice in seeing the evidence of intellectual maturity. While I have sincerely sought to persuade such students that philosophic interests are as serviceable within the ministry as out of it, nonetheless—having rendered my testimony—I am bound to state that it is against my principles to attempt to high-pressure, or to bully a mature mind, or to refuse to respect a decision that represents such a student's well-considered and responsible conviction.

Can a Christian Be a Philosopher?

There is one question I must deal with before I conclude. It is often claimed that true philosophy cannot be taught in an institution committed to the Christian world-view. It is even said that the genuinely philosophic point of view is inconsistent with professing the Christian faith. Such commitment, it is alleged, is incompatible with the intellectual independence, detachment, and open-minded tolerance that characterize the philosophic point of view. Faith, it is said, involves an invincible prejudice that necessarily contradicts philosophic tolerance. The religious believer is often charged with being philosophically dishonest because his answers have all been determined before the questions are asked. The gesture of candid inquiry, we are told, turns out to be only a pious fraud, a clever piece of dissembling. Now, this is tantamount to the charge that no convinced

Christian can be a philosopher—and that he is bound
to be a partisan propagandist for preconceived
opinions.

There is a grain of truth in this view insofar as it
involves a contrast between philosophical belief and
religious faith. These two are different attitudes. The
first is an intellectual assent to the truth of certain
propositions about the world, man, and God. The
second, religious faith, is a personal commitment of
our whole being to God; it is to love, trust, adore, and
obey God. These are not the same as believing certain truths about God, even though the beliefs and
the faith are inexorably connected.

Nevertheless, I would most emphatically deny that
holding the beliefs inherent in the Christian world-
view is incompatible with philosophical honesty.
Christian theism is certainly *one* of the hypotheses
concerning the nature of the universe that it is possible to entertain. It shares its status as a hypothesis
with many alternatives, such as Marxism, Platonism,
Evolutionary Naturalism, Pragmatism, Hegelianism.
It is as ridiculous to say there can be no Christian
philosophers as to say there can be no Hegelians, no
Kantians, no Pragmatists, no Materialists. Why
should it be professionally respectable to profess any
of the latter creeds, but be disrespectable to avow a
Christian world-view? *What marks a man's views
genuinely philosophical is not the creed itself, but
his ability to justify it rationally by adducing the kind
of evidence that sustains it.*

Now, I am fully persuaded that the evidence of science, art, history, and religious experience more fully vindicates the truth of Christian theism than any rival hypothesis. The Christian philosopher is prepared to assert that the overwhelming balance of probability—when *all*, not merely *partial*, lines of evidence are allowed their due weight—favors the theistic world-view of Christianity. Be this as it may, only a hopeless prejudice inspired by unconscious theophobia could deny that such is the honest and sincere conviction of countless intelligent persons. One encounters at times among philosophers the very unphilosophical attitude that it is professionally admirable to profess the most astonishing eccentricities—so long as they are not religious. But this is the voice of anti-religious dogmatism, not that of honest philosophy.

Granted, then, that there can be an honest Christian philosopher who entertains the theistic persuasion with a genuine and rationally defensible conviction, can he honestly teach such philosophy in a church-related college?

Now, it is evident that, due to institutional commitment to a Christian world-view, no Christian college would hire an atheist or a dialectical materialist to teach in its philosophy department. It would clearly violate the convictions of such a thinker and infringe the principle of academic freedom to employ him and then forbid him to expound and defend his views. It would, in fact, be dishonest for an atheist, knowing the institutional commitment, to accept employment in such an institution. On the other hand, the philosophic theist would find himself in rational agreement with the standpoint of the institution. He encounters no difficulty in expounding his views. He need not dissemble or infringe the principles of academic freedom, since his voluntary acceptance of the position presupposes his general agreement with the institutional position.

In claiming that a genuinely Christian philosophy is possible and that it can be taught with open-minded candor and genuine intellectual honesty, I claim to be doing no more than other teachers in other fields, who are bound to respect the claims of truth and of rational probability.

A mathematics teacher, while patient of the intellectual confusions of his student, in the end seeks to demonstrate the truth which, in mathematics, brooks no alternatives and no rivals. We would think it absurd to accuse the mathematician of being narrow-minded and dogmatic about the multiplication tables. Similarly, physicists are exponents of the truths of physics. They "intolerantly" reject "phlogiston" and "malicious animal magnetism." All this merely testifies to their scholarly mind, their intellectual integrity, and their genuine respect for truth.

Why, then, should it betoken a narrow intolerance in the Christian philosopher when he, too—having assessed fairly the measure of truth in alternative views—seeks to convince students of the validity of his convictions regarding the truth of religion and Christianity? He cannot be charged with taking advantage of his students. Students who elect to study in a Christian college are fairly warned that they will there encounter the Christian point of view. Those who find this point of view uncongenial can attend other institutions having no publicly avowed pre-commitments.

I conclude, therefore, that it is possible to be an honest Christian philosopher who can teach in a church college and maintain his intellectual integrity.

Of course, a Christian philosopher's method must itself be philosophical. It must employ the procedure of open inquiry, rational analysis, a fair consideration of opposing viewpoints, and a drawing of conclusions that are carefully qualified by the weight of the evidence. All this means that the philosopher is a teacher in the Socratic tradition, not an evangelist bent on emotional conversion.

I should add that I do not object to the evangelist so long as it is well understood that he *is* such and is about to give testimony. But even then the two methods cannot be wholly separated. The philosopher sometimes gets eloquent, and the evangelist gives reasons for his faith. Real life refuses to fit into our water-tight compartments. Truth itself, whether philosophic, scientific, or religious, has a profound affinity for personality. When truth meets the sensitive mind, a spiritual fire is apt to be kindled, and men begin speaking with tongues.

However, in this encounter, personality does not dominate the truth. Truth dominates the personality.

A teacher—whether of chemistry, or history, or philosophy, or religion—thus has the honor to become the loyal spokesman for the self-evidencing power of truth itself. So the truth must increase and the man must decrease. But this decrease, this return to intellectual humility, does not—strange to say—involve the derogation of personality. Rather, this loyalty to truth exalts man. Here, too, he only saves his life who consents to lose it—to the claims of truth. For all truth is God's truth, whether in science, art, mathematics, or theology. The servant of truth is the servant of God, whether he is aware of this or not. This is what it really means to be a teacher.

Chapter VII

RELIGIOUS EXPERIENCE
AND THE NURTURE OF
THE CHRISTIAN LIFE

Some years ago an able book was published with the arresting title, *Paths That Lead to God.* It is apparent from the theme of the book that there are various such paths. Perhaps it would be more accurate to say that there are various means of communication through which God invites us to know him and to trust him. These are the means which Christian higher education must use to attain its objectives.

Among these objectives, which include cultural, vocational, and recreational goals, is the primary one intended to permeate the student's attitude toward all the others—that, namely, of producing spirit-filled persons who may become the "leaven" and the "salt" of a secular and decadent society. The attainment of this goal requires the Christian college to produce persons who have not merely "knowledge of" God, but experimental "acquaintance with" God.

In order to understand how the college may facilitate this outcome, it is desirable to consider the meaning of religious experience. We take religious experience to be the obverse of what, from the divine side, is called revelation. What, then, is religious experience and how does it lead to knowledge of God? In answering this question it will be helpful at the outset to call attention to three ways of knowing.

Three Ways of Knowing

Two of these ways were designated by William James, the brilliant Harvard psychologist and philosopher of a generation ago, as "knowledge about" and "acquaintance with." I shall take the liberty of adding a third way of knowing and shall call it "experience of." Here, then, are three avenues of cognition—"experience of," "knowledge about," "acquaintance with."

"Experience of" means the knowledge involved and conveyed through sense-experience, through the perceptions that result from the stimulation of our eyes, our ears, and our other sense organs. Such sensations also arouse appropriate subjective feelings and emotions, such as pleasure, joy, delight, disgust, fear, etc. Thus our total experience is always a combination of objective perception and subjective feeling. (Perception is called objective because it reports the nature of the external object of thought, and feeling is called subjective because it reports the attitude of the knowing *subject* toward the external fact.) Now such ex-

perience is the foundation of all knowledge: of the world around us, of other people, of God. Unless these realities in some way entered into or aroused our experience, we would remain utterly unconscious of them.

After some previous experience has taken place, it is possible to extend knowledge beyond our immediate experience through the way of knowing called *"knowledge about."* This way of knowing is indirect, abstract, and conceptual. It consists in framing thoughts about things whether we perceive them or not. This is possible because of our ability to form ideas and to picture things in our imagination. Of course, any unperceived realities must be thought of as similar to the things we have experienced. If anything were absolutely different from anything we have ever experienced, if it had no resemblance at all to familiar things, we could not even think it or imagine it. All the abstract ideas we think with were originally conditioned upon, or derived from, experience.

These two ways of knowing, "experience of" and "knowledge about," exhaust our cognitive relations with the world of physical objects and impersonal facts. When we come to higher conscious beings, to other minds and especially to *persons*, a *third way* of knowledge comes into play. We shall call it *"acquaintance with."*

This kind of knowledge is not the perception of an *object*, but the recognition of another *subject*. It is the encounter of mind with mind. In its highest form it rests on mutual recognition and reciprocal communication. It may take place between a man and his dog, but not as adequately as between man and man. A still higher form is found in the communion between God and man. The higher forms of such "acquaintance with" depend on the completeness with which experience, purposes, and common tasks can be shared with each other. My dog, though he recognizes me, cannot understand me; God both recognizes me and understands me through and through. God can share his thoughts and purposes with man and solicit his response, just as man does with his fellow man. Hence, personal acquaintance between rational and creative persons is the highest level of such knowledge by "acquaintance with."

Before going on to point out the religious significance of these distinctions, let me point out that these ways of knowing are not necessarily mutually exclusive. They are dependent on each other and may all coexist together.

There can be no knowledge whatever without some original "experience of." There can be anticipatory "knowledge about" without any direct previous "experience with" the specific object under consideration, provided that such an object resembles something which we have previously experienced. When we deal with dead, inanimate, objects, "experience of" and hence "knowledge about" is as far as we can go. All scientific knowledge is of this kind.

There is a question as to the precise boundary that separates *"experience with"* and *"knowledge about."*

When I see the track of an electron in a Wilson cloud chamber, is my cognition of the electron "experience with" or only "knowledge about"? That it is *initially* an inferential entity postulated to account for many perceptible phenomena would indicate that here cognition begins as problematic "knowledge about." As long as such concepts remain on the level of general or universal description they abstract from concrete particularity and remain "knowledge about." Whenever, however, I am actively experiencing present sensations due to the action of some causal agency, I have "experience with."

The minimum description of this agent is "the entity now productive of this experience." Thus the criterion which distinguishes conceptual from perceptual cognition is whether the cognitive object is now actively controlling my consciousness because it is in interactive relations with me; or whether the object, being inaccessible in time, space, or causally ineffective or non-existent, is not now causally producing changes in my conscious experience.

Knowing Another Mind

Obviously, one's total knowledge of any fact varies. Of some facts I have only hearsay, second-hand "knowledge about." In some cases I have had previous but no *present* experimental knowledge. In many cases there is a mixture of experimental (past or present) and descriptive cognition. Such knowledge does not advance to the stage of "acquaintance with" unless that which is to be known is another mind. When "acquaintance with" does take place, however, it carries with it the previous "experience of" and "knowledge about." In other words, in personal acquaintance there always is a basis of previous *perceptual experience* and of *conceptual understanding*.

In this, the highest form of knowledge, all three ways of knowing are simultaneously present. We shall see presently that in acquaintance with God, all three ways of knowing are also simultaneously present.

Another thing needs to be pointed out. You may have noticed that another mind is not itself an *object* of sense perception. Another mind is an unseen *subject*. I cannot see your mind, hear your mind, touch your mind, taste your mind. But it is also true that I claim to have more than a second-hand report *about* your mind. When I talk with you, I find I have an immediate and unshakable conviction of standing in your personal presence. I know *you*, not facts about you. Your invisible personality becomes the object of my personal acquaintance. But this "acquaintance with" is neither a sensation nor a concept. We must say, therefore, that it is unique, *sui generis*, in that it involves a special capacity of mind: the ability, namely, to be intuitively aware of another subject.

How is this possible? Time does not permit detailed analysis of this problem of the psychology of personal perception. Like all the apparently simple things that we see or do every day, the familiar experience of recognizing our fellow man involves difficulties that defy analysis. Fortunately we can perform the feat without understanding it completely. However, something can be said about it. All personal recognition, or recognition of other minds, depends on the outward perceptible effects that minds produce.

These effects signal the presence of minds and their purposes. Even if telepathy occurs, it is certainly not the normal and dependable method of establishing personal acquaintance. Normal acquaintance with other minds is dependent on interpreting the outward, visible effects that minds produce in the external world. These physical effects are used as symbols. Without such effects visible to our senses, we would have no basis for the recognition of another personality, for nothing would excite our capacity for subjective intuition.

The Impersonal and the Expressive

An event in the outer physical world can be taken or understood in two distinct ways. It may be taken only as an *impersonal fact,* as a bare, meaningless item among passing events. Or, secondly, it may be taken as a *sign.* Now, a sign is something more than a bare fact. It is a fact having a meaning. A sign is a mode of personal expression, intended to express some intelligent purpose and to communicate it to another mind. Instead of being only an impersonal fact without significance, it becomes a significant or expressive fact. By expressing the presence and purpose of another mind, it mediates personal acquaintance.

Thus, for example, among your bodily activities the vibration of your vocal chords may be perceived only as physical events illustrating certain principles of physiology, or nerve action, or muscular reaction. But over and above this understanding of the vibration of your vocal chords as a physiological event, is the fact that these events constitute signs or words by means of which another person intuits the personal presence of your mind and comes to share your thoughts and experience.

These signs generally are words or verbal signs. But they need not be words. They may be gestures. They may be expressive acts and deeds. If you were dying of thirst in a desert and someone were to come along and silently place a flask of water to your lips, it would be an expressive deed. In fact, actions may frequently speak louder than words. Action signs may be more expressive than verbal signs.

Knowledge of God

Now all this applies to knowledge of God. God is another mind, in fact, he is the supreme Mind. Like human minds, God as subjective spirit is not perceptible to the senses.

We cannot see God with our eyes or hear him with our ears. Furthermore, unlike us human beings, God is not localized in a finite body, subject to the barriers of space and time. Man can directly control only his own body. God can control the whole of creation. God is omnipresent, everywhere present, everywhere active, ceaselessly preserving and upholding his created world.

Nothing whatever happens without this concurrence of God's creative power. "Whither shall I go from thy Spirit? Or whither shall I flee from thy presence? If I ascend to heaven, thou art there! If I make by bed in Sheol, thou art there! If I take the wings of the morning and dwell in the uttermost parts of the sea, even there thy hand shall lead me, and thy right hand shall hold me" (Ps. 139:7-10).

Now it is most important to note that this omnipresent, creative activity of God in the world can be taken in two ways: It can be taken as a series of impersonal or purely physical events, or it can be taken as sign language, as the *expressive activity of God.*

Nature is the action-language of God. Taken thus, all nature becomes, in biblical language, *a word of God.* It becomes the communication of his personal presence, in and through which we have a personal encounter with God. This is God's original creative revelation of himself. It is primordial and prevenient. It is universally available to all men and, as such, is the basis of that general and pervasive knowledge of God which appears, in distorted form, in all of man's religions and to which St. Paul refers in Romans 1: 19-20, "For what can be known about God is plain to them, because God has shown it to them. Ever since the creation of the world his invisible nature, namely, his eternal power and deity, has been clearly perceived in the things that have been made."

God, therefore, is not merely known logically or intellectually as an inference from facts taken impersonally. He is, indeed, thus known. And as the source and ground of all truth, *he is the ultimate objective of scientific knowledge.*

I do not disparage this intellectual approach to God. God has endowed our minds with rational capacities and subjected them to the irresistible authority of truth. We should, therefore, receive with gratitude all that can be known of God by such inference from scientific data. Such knowing, however, gets no farther than "knowledge about" God. It does not reach to a real "acquaintance with" God.

God, however, may be known as personally present, as an acquaintance, as one who reveals himself as *the living God in our personal experience.*

This kind of knowledge of God is what is meant by theologians and philosophers as "religious experience." This knowledge of God is intuitive and unreflective. It antedates philosophical and theological reflection. It is available to primitive, simple, and unsophisticated people. It is the basis of the spiritual convictions of poets and religious mystics. It is based not only on perceiving bare facts, but upon becoming aware of the meaning of the facts as the signs that communicate God's living presence and the expression of his will and purpose.

As soon as any fact acquires this meaning for a sensitive person, the fact ceases to be bare fact. *It has become a sign, carrying a meaning to be understood.* It has become *a word of God.*

Thus, for those having eyes to see and ears to hear, God's *words* may be processes in nature; they may be events of history, they may be the imperative duties of life; they may be the insights of poets and prophets; finally—and most important—God's greatest and final word may be, for those who receive the illumination of the spirit and the grace of faith, the personal presence of God in Jesus Christ, the eternal Son incarnate, the divine Word made flesh. Observe that these words of God are action words, not verbal words. Later, when sensitive and inspired prophets hear and understand these action words of God, they write them down. This record makes the revelation given in action words available to us in verbal form. Thus arises the written word of God, the Sacred Scriptures of the Old and the New Testaments.

God Reveals Himself

Let me reiterate, however, that the above three modes of cognition, *"experience of," "knowledge about,*" "*acquaintance with,*" are all singly or simultaneously involved in religious experience.

Revelation addresses itself to the whole man, not to some isolated "faculty." Revelation thus manifests the Revealer by expressing himself in intelligible meaning. This "intelligible meaning" is the connective tissue between spirits. It is the way spirit influences spirit, hence the way the supreme Spirit, God, influences our spirit: spirit thus answering to Spirit. This same intelligible meaning is the conductor of spiritual power, because its effect is not merely to convey information but to arouse personal awareness, and, in consequence, personal affection, loyalty, trust, and adoration.

This whole range of facts, taken together, including natural processes, historic events, consciousness of duty, the convictions of the prophet, the person of Jesus Christ, the words of the Bible, constitutes the word of God through which God reveals—not facts about himself, only—but himself as the living God in whose presence we stand and hear ourselves invited to know and to worship him.

Man's knowledge of God, whether primitive or mature, whether distorted by error or relatively true, whether biblical or extra-biblical, whether non-Christian or Christian—so far as it involves knowledge at all—rests thus upon God's revelation of himself. Intellectual knowledge about God is secondary, not primary. In the divine-human fellowship it is God who takes the initiative, not man.

We can discern, I believe, three phases of this revelation of God, three stages of the divine self-disclosure. God reveals himself as the sovereign Creator, as the righteous Judge, as the loving Redeemer and Sanctifier. The first two phases of revelation, which disclose God as sovereign Lord and righteous Will—as St. Paul shows in Romans 1—was granted in pre-Christian times universally to all men. It is known to men apart from the Christian revelation. It is truth so far as it is understood, but yet not the full and saving truth. It was not confined to Israel nor to the biblical record of Old Testament revelation.

Let us consider briefly the different forms that this universal personal self-manifestation of God takes in human experience.

As Creative Power[1]

We encounter God, in the first place, in experiencing the power that determines our existence, our status, our destiny. This power sets the limits and boundaries of my life. It controls me. I am powerless to control it. It confers existence upon me. It determines me as a human being, with human capacities, at this place, at this time, in this historic epoch, amidst this culture, this nation, with all my particular qualities and idiosyncrasies. These factors constitute

[1]The ensuing five sections paraphrase the trenchant insights of Paul Althaus, *Die Christliche Wahrheit*, Vol. I, Sections 6-10. C. Bertelsmann Verlag, Gutersloh, 1947. I gladly acknowledge my indebtedness to this great theologian.

my ineluctable fate which I am powerless to alter.
I can only accept them as the unchangeable and pre-
determined presuppositions of all my thinking, my
choosing, my doing. This power which establishes
my inescapable fate is recognized as neither arbitrary, for it is too orderly; nor as blindly automatic, for
it establishes my freedom even when it determines
me. Hence, as Schleiermacher correctly saw, we recognize this power on which we feel ourselves absolutely dependent, as the power of God. Our times
are in his hand. God is revealed as the determiner of
our destiny, the power-not-ourselves on which we
are absolutely dependent. We know ourselves as in
the hands of the Lord.

God as the Giver and Source of Good

God is personally revealed as the giver of all gifts.
I know myself blessed beyond all desert. The power
that determines my destiny endows me with the
capacities and the values that constitute my humanity. I have the power of thought, the desire for truth,
the zest for discovery, the joy of creation. We come
to know the values of the beautiful, the true, and the
good. We experience fellowship, and love, and the
opportunity to live in understanding and service. We
feel the elemental joy of life itself. As St. Peter puts
it in Acts 14:17, "Yet he did not leave himself without witness, for he did good and gave you from
heaven rains and fruitful seasons, satisfying your

hearts with food and gladness." "What hast thou which thou hast not received."

Thus is God known as the inexhaustible source of all good. "He who formed the eye, does he not see?" Shall the Giver of life not have life in himself? So is God known as the Power through whom we labor, as the final Good we seek, as the Truth to which knowledge aspires, as the Glory reflected in all beauty, as the great Companion for whom earthly love and filial affection inspire a heavenly longing and an infinite quest. God reveals himself as the Giver of every good and perfect gift, worthy of thanksgiving and adoration.

God Revealed in Moral Duty

God reveals himself, thirdly, in my consciousness of duty. I become aware, as Kant says, of categorical imperatives, of unconditional demands made upon me. To be sure, we first hear our fellow men making demands and issuing commands. We obey our parents, our superiors, our officers. But though we first encounter the commandments coming from men, we discern eventually that he who commands is ultimately not man, but a transcendent and righteous will.

We know this because we hear the command when no man calls. We hear it especially when it countermands the commandments of men. To hear this august imperative rebukes all human preten-

sions and sets us free from the tyranny of man. The
authority of the law is recognized as the authority
of the Lawgiver, the righteous will of God.

The obligation put upon me by this divine will
applies to the concrete circumstances of my life and
the details of my daily existence. It demands of me
truthfulness, cooperation, service, sacrifice even unto
death. And in loyalty to these obligations I know that
I alone can secure the worth and salvation of my
life. Thus does God reveal himself to me as the
Righteous and Holy One to whom I am responsible
and by whom I must be judged.

God Revealed in My Vocation

Closely related to this is another way that God
personally reveals himself. God is known as the one
who calls me to my task and guides me in its perform-
ance. He sets me in the midst of his creative ordi-
nances as parent, as churchman, as citizen, as a member of a profession or business. This is my vocation
and I must be loyal to it. I feel these obligations laid
upon me. My task chose me, not I it. This choice of
vocation, which I now know to be my imperative
duty, which in mysterious ways claimed me for its
own, contrary to all my anticipations and predictions,
I come to know as God guiding my life.

I see that I am a member of his flock. "The Lord
is my shepherd, I shall not want. . . . . he leads me
beside still waters; he restores my soul. He leads me

in paths of righteousness for his name's sake. Even though I walk through the valley of the shadow of death, I fear no evil; for thou art with me."

This profound sense of vocation, this conviction of being called to a task, this consciousness of a "providence that shapes our ends, roughhew them as we may," we come to know as God guiding our lives and giving them meaning, direction, and fruitfulness.

God Revealed in Intellect and Beauty

Finally God reveals himself in sharing with us the richness of his intellect and his love of beauty. This is the personal and mystical form that scientific or artistic interest may take. The world of nature is not only a set of facts to be reported, analyzed, or systematized. It is also an expression of intelligence and a communication of thought. "God," said Sir Isaac Newton, "was the first geometrizer. Men but think God's thoughts after him." In that he endows us with a rational mind, with an intelligence that can in part grasp the intelligibility of nature, God invites us to share in his mind, in the profundity of his thought, in his creative ingenuity, in the inexhaustible fecundity of his divine imagination.

So, too, the beauty of nature reveals to us the divine artist sharing with us his esthetic experience in the glory of sunsets, the vast loneliness of the sea, the majesty of the starry heavens, the color and the

fragrance of a flower. "Consider the lilies of the
field," says Jesus, ". . . even Solomon in all his glory
was not arrayed like one of these. . . . If God so
clothes the grass of the field, . . . will he not much
more clothe you, O men of little faith?" So it is God
who clothes the world with splendor and beauty and
inspires the ardor of creative thought.

The acquaintance with God which results from
these various media of revelation is, as we have said,
pre-Christian, extra-biblical, and universally available. In saying this we are but following St. Paul
and other biblical writers. To be sure, there are eyes
that see not and ears that hear not. There are those
who but dimly perceive God as manifest in these experiences. There are those who even deny the reality
of God and his relevation. And so this knowledge of
God, real even when it is but imperfectly appre-
hended, tends to be corrupted, distorted, and obscured by the vanity and evil lusts of men. Men "ex-
change the glory of the immortal God for images
resembling mortal man," and "exchanges the truth
about God for a lie" and for the expression of a "base
mind." God has not left himself without a witness to
the nations.

But genuine as his universal revelation is, valid as
is the creative and the ethical word, it is either un-
heeded by sinful man, or distorted into dreadful
superstition, or corrupted into obscene idolatry. The
general revelation of God as Creator and as righteous Judge, therefore, is incomplete and spiritually

inadequate without the final revelation of God's redemptive love.

God Revealed in Redemptive Love

Through the inspiration of the prophets, God granted to Israel a much purer and more adequate revelation of himself, both as Creator and as the Righteous One. This revelation was given as the historic fulfillment of God's saving purpose in Jesus Christ. Thus the revelation recorded in the Bible includes the truth of such general revelation as may be found in non-biblical religions but passes far beyond it in disclosing God's loving-kindness and tender mercies and the promise of redemption and renewal through the coming Messiah. Because the Messiah, God's anointed, was to enter history through the historic and religious culture of Judaism, Israel became the covenant people with a unique and exclusive vocation as the means of realizing God's redemptive purpose.

This latter, the revelation of God's redemptive love, was given in its fulness in Jesus Christ and the Gospel of divine forgiveness through divine suffering and atonement for human sin. This, the final revelation of the Gospel, is given through Jesus Christ alone and is made available to us by the Holy Scriptures of both the Old and New Testaments. It discloses the fully saving truth of the length, and breadth, and depth of the love of God in Christ Jesus.

Nothing can surpass or outmode this supreme act of God. Nothing can require it to be done again. It is final, complete, and all-sufficient for its purpose. As a saving act it is eternally and universally effective. As a final proof of God's love toward us, who are most unworthy and in no way deserving of such divine mercy, it is unsurpassable and unfathomable.

God, through the various modes of relevation which we have thus considered, seeks to disclose himself to us in all forms of human experience and to solicit our response, our love, and our loyalty. Yet he does so without overwhelming us by the majesty of his absolute and unveiled presence. What mortal can look upon God and live?

Yes, God reveals himself. But God does not obtrude himself upon man by force. He does not coerce or psychologically intimidate man's mind and man's conscience. He indeed makes himself available. He is not far from any one of us. Yet it is also true, as Jesus said, that only he who seeks shall find, and only to him who knocks will the door be opened. God is never obvious. He is a God of paradoxes. He reveals himself, but he remains hidden. He is both *Deus revelatus* and *Deus absconditus*. He thunders in the still small voice. He is the omnipotent Creator who shows his supreme power by dying for his creature. His glory shines brightest in humiliation and service. God takes the initiative, but he does not answer unless we freely seek, and freely knock, and freely grope after him, if haply we shall find him.

The Nurture of the Christian Life

We have now to inquire whether the Christian college, understood as an academic community composed predominantly of Christians, can effectually mediate religious experience as thus described, and so produce those "spirit-filled persons who may become 'leaven' and 'salt' in a secular decadent society."

Now there seems no reason to believe that spiritual influence and the "intelligible meaning" which conveys personal revelation is to be limited to one means only. If we are to love God with all our heart, with all our soul, with all our mind, that is, with all our powers, we may well believe that an appeal to religious affection, to dynamic commitment, and to intellectual insight are all proper means of Christian nurture and at the disposal of the Christian college.

I therefore believe that, in the first place, the intellectual approach to religion is thoroughly justified. Truth is spiritually persuasive. True knowledge of God mediates the presence of God and leads to religious experience. The Christian college does right, then, to maintain a "Department of Religion" as a subject-matter discipline. But if so, religious knowledge should be taught with the same systematic and scholarly rigor, with the same scrupulous respect for new truth, and with the same regard for contemporary relevance as any other subject in the college program. There is a strange notion that theology is the special prerogative of the theological seminary.

But if a college student can be expected to master a scholarly textbook on biology, geology, psychology, not to mention nuclear physics or differential calculus, why should he not study theology? The reason the student frequently looks down on the religion department is its tendency to intellectual flabbiness, its adolescent approach, its process to substitute pious sentiment for incisive thinking.

Let the college, then, take Christianity seriously and teach Christian theology on a mature level. Of course, theology is a broad terrain and in practice must be represented by specialized courses. Some of the most important of these would be "The Bible as the Literature of Redemptive Revelation," "Fundamental Christian Doctrines," "Principles of Christian Ethics," "Contemporary Apologetics," "The Christian Approach to Vital Contemporary Issues."

The Supremacy of Personal Influence

But the religious objectives of the Christian college must include also, as far as possible, *the* integral nurture of Christian life and character. Such nurture attempts to encourage an existential response of personal communion with God instead of an intellectual response only. At this point the Christian college encounters its most delicate problem.

Men cannot be commanded to worship. Worship must be inspired by inner desire. The college may encourage the practice by precept and example and may provide facilities and opportunities of various kinds. But, in the final analysis, the student must be drawn into the fellowship of worship by personal influence. Worship is the heart's joyful obeisance to the infinite "worth" of God. It presupposes personal awareness of standing in the presence of the living God, the Author of my life and my salvation, and who evokes, therefore, the response of faith, contrition, repentance, gratitude, obedience, and adoration. Worship occurs in the form of private prayer, devotion, and meditation, either individually or in groups, or in the form of public services.

Worship is authentic, however, only when it expresses the free and spontaneous response of the worshiper. It is a form of "seeking" and "knocking," and God has promised that "he who seeks will find," and "to him who knocks the door shall be opened."

It should obviously be the aim of the Christian college that all who join its fellowship shall receive this divine enrichment of personal life. To this end the student must be gently inducted into the radiance of Christ.

While guidance in so-called techniques and the availability of suitable means, such as Bibles, prayer books, manuals of devotion, private chapels, scheduled hours, and the like, all have their value, it must be pointed out that the real medium of spiritual influence is Spirit-filled persons. The Christian virtues of love, patience, humility, courtesy, gentleness, and service are made appealing when embodied in personal character. The fellowship of such persons creates the spiritual atmosphere which contagiously permeates all its members.

This observation brings us to the crux of the problem. Since the faculty is the more or less permanent nucleus of the college community, the Christian atmosphere of the college and the intensity of its radiance must reflect largely the spiritual stature of the members of the faculty. Both academically and spiritually *a college can be no better than its faculty.* One could paraphrase Archimedes and say, "Give me a faculty big enough [intellectually and spiritually] and I will move the world." Hence the chief duty of a college president is to find a good faculty—a group of dedicated persons who are both scholars and Christians. It is a formidable task, and only a man of imperturbable idealism, who is nevertheless inured to sad disappointment, and who can muster infinite patience with mediocrity, should attempt to be a college president.

We are thus brought back, in the end, to Mark Hopkins on one end of a log and a student on the other. The combination is the essence of a good college, a Christian college. Given Mark Hopkins and the student, all else is expendable window-dressing. *The personal equation is supreme.*

I have seen many admirable plans, courses, curricula—on paper. I have helped to construct them. They are no better than the persons that implement them. Be they ever so good, modern, up-to-date, the latest thing, buttressed by mountains of experimental statistics, marvelously exemplified elsewhere—if they are administered by mediocrities, the results will be mediocre.

For a Christian college to succeed, its faculty should be made up of Robert Speers, Frank Laubachs, Albert Schweitzers. It is as simple as that. Where are the men equal to this task? Let us pray the Lord of the harvest that he may find men and women to work in his vineyard!